Never mind the gap

To the memory of Jack and Emily King who showed me how to grandparent well

Acknowledgement

This book could never have been written without the help of many people including the children and families, including grandparents, with whom I have worked over the years. A special word of thanks needs to go to those agencies that have helped in the gathering of information for this book — Age Concern, The Mothers' Union, The National Stepfamily Association, the Faith in the Future Group of the National Christian Education Council and to those people who completed questionnaires. I would also like to thank Elizabeth Bruce and Liam Purcell for their help in turning a manuscript into a book and Martin Lambourne for his encouragement.

The preparation and production of this book have been supported by a donation to the Faith in the Future *project.*

Never mind the gap

A book for grandparents

Joan King

Cover design by Image-On Artworks, Hull

Published by:
National Christian Education Council
1020 Bristol Road
Selly Oak
Birmingham
B29 6LB

British Cataloguing-in-Publication Data:
A catalogue record for this book is available from the British Library.

ISBN 0-7197-0934-2
First published 1999
©1999 Joan King

Designed and typeset by National Christian Education Council
Printed and bound by Biddles, Guildford, UK

Contents

Introduction

Welcome to *Never Mind the Gap*, a book for grandparents, prospective grandparents and those who might never have grandchildren of their own but who may become significant older people in the lives of children without grandparents.

It is a striking thought that on first becoming a grandparent most people still have twenty, thirty, forty active years of life ahead of them. The images of grandparents as out of touch, old and infirm do not reflect the realities of grandparents' lives today. Times have changed and there are more grandparents alive than ever before. This book is for them and it has been written because so many of them have asked for a book or resource. To quote some of them: 'The world is a very different place from when we grew up and from when we were parenting our own children.'

For years people have talked about a 'generation gap' between older people and the younger generations. Usually this gap has been seen negatively — the different generations have their own ways, will not understand each other, will not share interests and will not want to do things together. My experience of working with children and families for over thirty years made me question some of these assumptions. Numerous children and young people have talked about their grandparents and the overwhelming impression has been that they have warm, positive thoughts about them. Some may experience them as distant, sadly a few may have experienced them as abusive but the majority, well, they just love them. They talk of visits, of doing everyday things together, of being 'spoiled' (just a little), of laughing and playing, of being helped out of a crisis in the teenage years. With so many children speaking warmly of grandparents I wondered whether there is any such thing as a generation gap between them.

Introduction

The answer is that there are two and it is the two-generation distance between children and grandchildren that can make their relationship so special — that is, if grandparents choose to invest time in that relationship. Read on and I hope that you will see some of the benefits of the two-generation gap.

The book is arranged in three sections: the first raises issues for grandparents, the second explores the world of children and the third explores some things that grandparents can do to sustain a relationship with grandchildren and to support them as they learn and grow. Each section is divided into chapters. Within each chapter is one or more sections headed *Take Ten*. These sections are designed to help you to reflect on what you have read and to make some discoveries for yourself. Most will take about ten minutes to do, some will take more. You may find it helpful to have a notebook and pen alongside you as you read so that you can record your findings from the *Take Ten* sections as well as any personal thoughts or discoveries that you make along the way.

By way of guidance, the word 'child' is used in this book to mean those who are still in primary school, which in most areas includes all under twelve years of age. 'Young children' are those under eight years of age and the very young are under five with reference being made to toddlers and babies. That is probably all the information that you need before starting to read. So find that notebook and pen and begin.

Note:
Much of the information for this book has been gathered from questionnaires completed by parents, grandparents and children solely for use in this book. While quotations are accurate, in most cases names have been changed to avoid identification.

Section 1:
Grandparents and grandparenting

Memories

World War II had just ended. There was great excitement in our household as we waited for Grandad to arrive. He was coming a long way — two hundred miles on a steam train. I was four at the time and could not conceptualize the distance. What I remember are the feelings that surrounded his visit — awe, joy, happiness. There was a sense of mystery about this man who was obviously very important, especially to Dad. He brought gifts and lots of 'news'. I remember listening in wonder as he told stories about people whom my parents obviously knew and loved (my aunts, uncles and cousins who had been separated through the war) and I remember sensing that in some way I was linked to them.

At the time I did not realize that Grandad was my living ancestor, a blood tie. I remember him as kind and gentle with me, loved and respected by my parents. Cruelly, within a year of his visit and before we had been on our family holiday to stay with him, Grandad was killed in a road accident. By the age of five I was grandorphaned.

Both my grandmothers died years before I was born. My maternal grandfather, with whom we lived, died after a long illness when I was fourteen months old. Yet, I feel that all my grandparents have always been there because they were part of my parents' lives. They are members of the family that stretches into the past. They have helped me to know my place of belonging in my family history and have enabled me to have a strong sense of my own roots, largely through the family legends, stories, photographs and artefacts that they left behind.

When I started school I discovered that there were other children who did not have grandparents but I was more fortunate than many of them. There were elders in my family who took on some of the grandparenting roles. Most of them were warm people whose legacy to me is a bank of good memories — of laughter and fun, of doing things together, of valuing and being valued. However, some elders were more distant, perhaps less comfortable with children, and sometimes plain grumpy. At an early age I began to discover that older people are unique individuals. Some I enjoyed being with more than others!

Reflecting on my experiences I can see that all the older people in my life as a child and teenager were important influencers. Whether the influences were positive or negative I learned from them. I wanted either to be like particular elders or different from them. As I consider my life now, I am aware that my elders have been there through life's journey perhaps unaware of the impact they have had. Most of them simply accepted me.

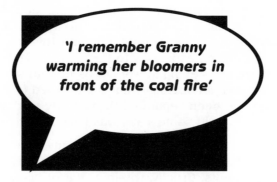

'*I remember Granny warming her bloomers in front of the coal fire*'

Your experience of being grandparented will be different from mine. However, both of us will no doubt be influenced by our experiences as we approach being grandparents (or honorary grandparents) ourselves. Therefore, before considering the subject of contemporary grandparenting further it may be worth pausing to recall some experiences and the impact they made.

Take Ten

You may like to have a pen and some paper with you.

1. Be still. Breathe deeply and clear your mind.
   Remember some of the older people in your childhood — your grandparents, elders or honorary grandparents.
   Think of events that you shared with them. Think of images you associate with them. Identify the feelings that go with the events and images.

   * How did you feel about your grandparents? Note down some of your thoughts, positive and negative.

   * What did you learn from your grandparents and in what ways have you been influenced by them?

2. Leave your childhood behind and think of yourself now. Think of your current circumstances. Imagine that your grandparents and other older people about whom you have been thinking are with you.

   * What would you like to say to them?

   * What would you want to thank them for?

   * What would you ask them?

   * What would you tell them that you found unhelpful?

3. As someone who is, or is about to be, a grandparent or elder consider:

   * In what ways would you want to copy or be like your grandparents or elders while grandparenting?

   * In what ways would you want to be different from your grandparents?

   Write a note to yourself as a reminder of your answers to these questions.

Of course, you and I were grandparented at particular times in history. In my case, growing up through the 1940s and 50s I was parented and grandparented through some austere and difficult war years into years of great hope when the political slogans told us that 'we have never had it so good'. Materially things improved. Most of us lived in fairly stable families — I knew of one school friend whose parents divorced and whose maternal grandmother became a co-parent. Other peers lost their dads in the war and again their grandparents seemed to take very active roles in their upbringing. By the time we were young adults, enjoying the swinging sixties, most of my friends had lost their grandparents through death while others had absent grandparents living miles away.

Today's grandparents are pioneers. Their context for grandparenting is different. Yes, people have been grandparenting for generations and have fulfilled some traditional roles through time, but no other generation has faced the unique challenges that life in a western culture poses at this point in history. It is true that some of what has been learned from our own grandparents and elders will give us useful insights and models but grandparents today will experience their role differently. Greater awareness of self, of changing culture and the contexts in which grandchildren live will help grandparents to face the future with increased confidence. The rest of this book sets out to assist you in experiencing the grandparenting stage of your life as an adventure through which you, your grandchildren and adult children may continue to grow and learn.

Prayer

Lord,
Thank you for the memories

— of my own childhood

— of those older people who were part of it.

Help me to learn from those memories
and be with me as I begin (or continue)
the adventure of grandparenting.

First grandchild, new grandparent

'You're going to be a grandparent.' Imagine that your son or daughter has telephoned with this message. You have never been a grandparent before. How would you respond to this news? It may be something that you have been longing to hear or the very idea may fill you with dread. You have seven months or so to prepare for the event and to think about your prospective new role.

Some people rehearse for years what it will be like to be a grandparent. They dream of the day when they will hold the baby, and have grandparent status and a new role with children. As one new grandmother told me, 'I couldn't wait to have a grandchild. It is so exciting. I've told my daughter not to worry about child care. My husband and I will do that. He's taking early retirement and looking forward to spending time with the baby — time he did not have for our own daughter.'

Most parents want to become grandparents. For instance, in a study of 250 grandparents in the United States in 1993 nearly all respondents (96%) said that they had wanted grandchildren[1]. However, on hearing the news that they were actually to be grandparents their reactions were not always so positive. Some were pleased and others not. Imagine responses from those who hear that their sixteen-year-old daughter is about to become a teenage single mother; those who hear that their son and his wife are to be parents after having difficulty conceiving a child, or those who suspect that their grandchild has been conceived to try to save a troubled marriage, or those who hear of a planned pregnancy and those who hear of an 'accidental' one. Circumstances affect initial responses.

I have heard of some people who are so anxious to become grandparents that they put great pressure on their adult children to produce them. 'My brother nags his son to produce a grandchild,' wrote one respondent to my questionnaire. Unfortunately such pressure is likely to affect adversely his relationship with his son and daughter-in-law. Most couples today can choose whether to have children or not but it is their decision and not that of 'wannabe' grandparents. It is also worth remembering that increasing numbers of couples (one in six) are unable to conceive a child and may not yet have told hopeful prospective grandparents of their struggle. So be sensitive.

While many people feel driven to become grandparents others do not know whether or not they want grandchildren until they have them. 'Considering I had not been particularly "broody" about having grandchildren I was surprised by the depth of my feeling of overwhelming joy.' For other people the news that they are to be grandparents comes at the wrong time. Yes, they want to have grandchildren but not yet. They are facing too many changes or transitions in their own lives and are not ready for the role or status of grandparenthood. Doreen expressed this eloquently:

'I just wasn't ready. The big 5-0 was looming. I had a responsible job involving lots of change and my husband had died just a few years previously. It was too soon. During the pregnancy I was not interested in the prospective birth. I wasn't ready for the next stage of my life.'

When her granddaughter was born, however, Doreen's feelings changed.

'I got involved. Shortly after the birth my daughter-in-law became ill and I helped to care for the baby for two weeks. In that time we bonded and I found that I loved her very much. I felt very protective towards her — I think the protectiveness was because her mother was so ill.'

At that point it was as if Doreen's desire to grandparent was kicked into action.

Take Ten

Reflect on these questions and note down your thoughts. (You may need to adjust them to fit your circumstances e.g. the first question may become, 'How would you feel...').

* ✴ How did you feel about the prospect of becoming a grandparent or elder?
* ✴ Were you keen and ready to be a grandparent or was the timing unhelpful to you? If so, why?
* ✴ What else was happening in your life at the time?
* ✴ What was the context of your family at the time (e.g. your elderly parents were moving into sheltered accommodation)?

As we have seen, before the birth there are positive and negative responses to the idea of being a grandparent. Some people are influenced by their images of grandparents, others feel that they are too young or they have too many responsibilities. Some are thrilled with the news. Once the baby arrives, however, the new grandchild is usually welcomed and loved no matter what the initial reaction to prospective grandparenthood has been. Here are some of the responses of people quoted earlier in this chapter. They were asked to describe their feelings when their first grandchild was born.

'Thankfulness, pleasure and wonderment.'

'Excited, delighted and very privileged.'

'Gratitude for a safe delivery.'

'Overwhelming love.'

'Excited and anxious for my grandson's future, spiritually and in other ways.'

Meeting a new grandchild can indeed be a spiritual moment — a moment when you see a new life entrusted by God to the care of the parent(s), the extended family and community. And within that extended community, grandparents have a special place. Many people agree that the child/grandparent relationship is second only to the parent/child relationship in terms of its mutual benefit to adult and child.

17

First grandchild, new grandparent

Becoming a grandparent for the first time marks a milestone in life. Parents move up the generational ladder to become grandparents. Their adult children become parents and those in the previous grandparent generation become great-grandparents. The family is changed, it is restructured when the grandchild is born. At this point most grandparents begin to function as grandparents and to develop their identity as family elders. According to Arthur Kornhaber[1] grandparents have two tasks at this point in their own development. The first is internal. They have to accept the child into their lives and themselves in their new role. It is at this stage that some people shift the focus of their lives away from work, career, appearance or financial success to be more people- and family-orientated. For many, simple activities such as baby-sitting and caring for a child become real pleasures. One person put it this way, 'I was given a new lease of life ... my life had a new meaning.'

The second task is to work with the family situation — the relationships, location (geographical distance between households), and life situations. Grandchildren are born into dynamic families. While the grandparents may have a deep desire to grandparent, the circumstances of the family may affect what they are able to do. For instance, a person becoming a grandparent for the first time at the age of eighty is likely to have less physical energy than a person becoming a grandparent at the age of forty; a new grandparent whose grandchild is overseas will have to learn to grandparent from a distance.

The state of the relationships between the child's parent(s) and grandparents will also have a bearing on opportunities for active grandparenting. Sometimes the birth of a grandchild can provide an opportunity for strengthening or even repairing a relationship. One grandparent wrote:

> 'The birth of my grandson was highly significant. For two years I had been estranged from my son but when the baby came along he said that he did not want to deprive his son of his grandmother. It was as if there was a crack in the door (the barrier) that was between us. Now my son and I have established a new relationship. In a way my grandson salvaged our relationship.'

For others the shifts in relationship are less dramatic, perhaps more subtle:

'I have a very caring son and there has been little change in our relationship.'

'We talk about different things like the progress of the baby. She will ask for advice from time to time (something she did not do before) and I am learning to wait to be asked.'

There may be other aspects of the family dynamic with which you have to come to terms in order to grandparent well in your family context. It may be that you have deeply held beliefs about child-rearing within marriage, that are rooted in your own faith, and your grandchild has been born to a couple who cohabit, or to your daughter who has chosen to remain single. Such realities must be faced and worked with if grandparents are to grandparent effectively. Most parents, whatever their marital status, appreciate sensitive support and are glad when their child's grandparents offer love to the grandchild and become significant in his or her life. In such cases communication is key between parents and grandparents. Consulting with the parents and planning together how best to support and fulfil your grandparenting role, while taking into account your life stage and personal circumstances, will no doubt be helpful to all of you.

Take Ten

Reflect on these questions. The first group of questions is for prospective grandparents and elders and the second group for those who have already become grandparents/elders.

1. ✻ How do you think you will feel when you meet your first grandchild?
   ✻ How might your life change when you become a grandparent or elder?
   ✻ What might be done to help you to recognize that you have moved up a generation?
2. ✻ What were your reactions and feelings when you met your first grandchild?
   ✻ In what ways has your life changed because you have become a grandparent?
   ✻ What are the family circumstances with which you have to work?
   ✻ What has, or has not, helped you to move into your new generation and to function as a grandparent?

19

First grandchild, new grandparent

It is usually helpful to mark a milestone in life with an event that will help to make real what has happened to us. When the reality of the new stage of life has not been accepted, a grandchild can be robbed of a grandparent. 'My Mummy has a Mummy but I do not have a grandmother'[1] because Grandma feels that she is too young to be a grandmother and so does not function as one. Equally a grandparent may feel robbed of the grandparent status if the great-grandparent does not shift up a generation.

'Often I do not feel like a true grandmother. My mother has always enjoyed her grandmother status in the family and she does not want to share it or relinquish it to me.'

When your first grandchild is born all generations face a new stage in their lives. Marking the milestone may help all to recognize their new positions in the family. There are different ways of doing this. Some people find that a thanksgiving service for the gift of the child, a naming ceremony, or an infant baptism in which all make promises to do their part in the care and upbringing of the child, is sufficient. While the focus of the service may be on the child and the parent's need for support from God and his people during their child-rearing years, the other generations involved may be helped through the service to realize that their child or grandchild has moved into the parent generation. This realization may, in turn, enable them to recognize or accept their own move into a new generation and to function in their new role.

One couple I know designed their own thanksgiving for the birth of their child. Their son is called Evan so they planned a celebration called 'Evan on Earth'. In the dedication of their son to God they gave grandparents a role. Evan's grandfather spoke these words slightly adapted from Numbers 6.24-26.

'Evan, the Lord look kindly on you and give you peace.
My grandson, the Lord bless you.'

The simple insertion of the words 'My grandson', spoken in public, provided the marker. Other people have found that markers for them have come when they have received cards congratulating them on becoming a grandparent or great-grandparent. Seeing the written words has helped to make real for them their shift into a new generation.

Take Ten

* How did, or would, you mark the milestone of becoming a grandparent for the first time? What did, or would, you find helpful?

* Imagine that some friends of yours are to become grandparents for the first time. Plan or design an event, rite or liturgy that will help them and others like them to mark this milestone in their lives.

Becoming a grandparent gives us the opportunity to grow personally. All new experiences can do that. In subsequent years other grandchildren may be added to the family. They may be the younger siblings of your first grandchild, or the children, step-children, adopted or foster children of your other sons and daughters. Each child will be different. Each set of parents will be different. In each case family circumstances, including relationships, will affect how you grandparent. For example, the role that you take with your son's child may be different from the one that your daughter wants you to have with her child. Nevertheless, while every grandchild may be loved but possibly grandparented differently by you, it is the milestone of becoming a grandparent for the first time that is likely to make the greatest impact on your personal growth.

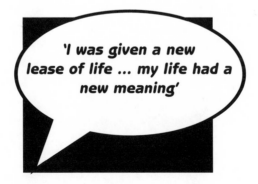

'*I was given a new lease of life ... my life had a new meaning*'

The prayer of a first-time grandparent

Lord,
I am amazed by this child —
so tiny, so perfect, so lovely
and so dependent on my child.

I had forgotten what it is like,
holding your baby for the first time,
but the memories are flooding back –
the joy, the love, the awful responsibility
and the tiredness.

The child that I held is now the parent
of this child — my grandchild.
Thank you for the gift of this grandchild
and help me to parent and grandparent well.

Reference

1 Kornhaber A, *Contemporary grandparenting* (SAGE Publications 1996), pp 69, 77.

Today's grandparents

As the twentieth century dawned, life expectancy for men was forty-eight and for women fifty-two. If you reached your mid-forties you were usually an 'old grandparent'. Not so today! When our first grandchild is born we probably have thirty or forty years of active life ahead of us.

Submissions to a survey by the Mothers' Union revealed some pictures of grandparents early in this century. 'Grandma wore black' and 'Grandfather was the head of the household.' Grandmas featured more in the submissions than grandfathers who were rarely part of the memory. A view of a rigid, God-fearing family structure emerged. Some fifty or so years later we were being grandparented. As we saw in the last chapter, our grandparents and other elders left us with a series of memories and images that we carry with us. They inform our understanding of the role of grandparents and our expectations of ourselves as grandparents and elders. Many of us may carry a stereotyped image of what the perfect or model grandparent is like and feel that we cannot live up to it. So what are contemporary grandparents like and what are they doing? Here are three examples.

Lydia is in her mid-fifties and took early retirement a year ago although she remains on the supply register for primary teaching and has been called on fairly regularly. She lives with her husband, Ken, who also took early retirement. They visit the local swimming pool at least once a week and are actively involved in the local church, especially in visiting and caring capacities. Lydia also helps with the planning of all-age worship and Ken heads up the welcome team. Their three adult children are married and they have five grandchildren with another on the way. Two grandchildren live nearby and Lydia and Ken see them almost daily. They enjoy being part of their lives and having time to do everyday things with these two children who are both pre-schoolers. The other grandchildren live about two hundred miles away. Two are in primary school and the third will be starting next year. Lydia and Ken visit about twice a year, talk regularly on the telephone and enjoy having their oldest daughter, son-in-law and three children to stay with them in school holidays. The expected grandchild will be the first born to Lydia and Ken's youngest son who lives about fifty miles away. He and his partner have chosen to cohabit which was a disappointment to Lydia and Ken but they think their son and his partner will make good parents and hope that they will be given the opportunity of supporting them in bringing up the latest member of the family.

Nina is an older grandparent. She is in her mid-seventies and nursed her husband for a couple of years with cancer. He died three years ago. Gradually Nina is rebuilding her life. During this period her son has supported her, visited regularly and enabled her to take a holiday. She has a large circle of friends, mainly from the church, and makes the coffee for the mums who attend the Toddler Group. Her son married quite young. He and his wife were career people who chose not to have children. Over the years they drifted apart and finally divorced. At forty her son remarried and Nina immediately gained two step-grandchildren, now in their teens. She has worked hard at 'being there' for these young people and is pleased that they often use her as a 'sounding board'. This year her son and his wife had a baby — a girl who Nina says is a delight and has given her a new lease of life. She feels that her daughter-in-law needs a good deal of support and wishes she had more energy so that she could increase the practical support she can offer.

Bernard and Elaine both work and enjoy their jobs, though if pushed they would say that family comes before work. Elaine worked for most of her children's school years though she had a break while they were young. Now their two children are parents themselves and Bernard and Elaine are grandparents to three children all under the age of eight. Two grandchildren live within ten miles and Bernard and Elaine visit them about once a fortnight. Sometimes they baby-sit. The children love it when they come for weekend sleepovers. They see their third grandchild, who lives fifty miles away, about twice a term — either he comes with his parents for a meal and 'catch-up' or they visit and take in a Chinese take-away. One of Bernard and Elaine's great joys, now that they have finished paying off the mortgage on their house, is that they can fund a family holiday. They usually take a large cottage or a couple of caravans near a beach and enjoy having fun with the children and seeing the world through young eyes as they explore the beach, play or watch a video together. Sometimes they care for the children in the evening, read bedtime stories, etc. while the parents have an evening out. In this way they feel that they are supporting their own children. They remember having little time together in their earlier parenting years when there were no baby-sitters on hand.

Take Ten

* You are a 'today' grandparent or elder. In what ways is your grandparenting situation the same as, and in what ways is it different from, those above?

* Supposing your story or situation was written for inclusion above, what would you include? Write a description of yourself as a contemporary grandparent and include some detail about your children and grandchildren. If you prefer you could use cartoons or drawings instead of a written description.

Black may be a fashionable, even smart, colour for grandmothers to wear today just as it was for our predecessors in the Mothers' Union study, but times have changed. Our grandchildren are being born into a variety of fluid, sometimes ruptured, family situations in which grandparents feature as lively, active people though sometimes they have to grandparent from a distance. No doubt, to the children, grandparents will be 'old' because to many of them anyone over twenty is old, but their pictures and images of what it means to be a grandparent in the 1990s will be quite different from those of grandchildren earlier in the century. Imagine Grandma going to the line-dancing group with you or, as in the case of one child I know, actually teaching the group he attends! Today's grandparents, who on the whole are fit, active and well, are in a position to provide positive models that will help grandchildren to grow up unafraid of their own ageing processes. They will be part of their grandchildren's lives for many years and will have to adjust relationships as children grow into teenagers, young adults and adults in mid-life — but more of that later.

Today's grandparents

On 20 September 1997, Age Concern England issued a press release giving facts and figures about the 'big picture' concerning grandparenting today so, having looked at our individual situations, let's look at the findings of an Age Concern study of relationships across the generations. Here are some of the points made.

'The extended family is alive and well, with grandparents staying highly involved in the lives of their grandchildren.'

'Britain's 16.5 million grandparents provide invaluable care and support for young families. Most see their grandchildren on a regular basis and some even e-mail to keep in touch.'

'Grandparents generally still live close enough to be very involved with grandchildren and make a valuable contribution towards their overall wellbeing ... but twenty-six per cent have at least one grandchild living more than one hundred miles away.'

'Just under one third of all adults (three quarters of over sixty-fives and ten per cent of people aged fifty-five and under) are grandparents and the average number of grandchildren is four.'

'Despite increasing mobility, almost three quarters (73%) of grandparents live less than ten miles from at least one of their grandchildren... Those in higher income groups tend to live further away from their grandchildren... Whatever the distance there is still a high level of contact... Eighty-six per cent of grandparents have regular contact with their grandchildren and a quarter write letters.'

Take Ten

It appears that today's grandparents are highly involved in the lives of their grandchildren. They offer them love and significant relationships. Like grandparents in the past they will have an impact on their grandchildren's lives now and in the future, leaving them with experiences and memories, both positive and negative, that will influence their development and possibly their life choices.

It is likely that your grandchildren are more interested in what kind of person you are than in what you do with them. Think about yourself and your involvement with your grandchildren and then think about these questions.

* How would you like your grandchildren to remember you?

* What images and memories of you do you hope they will take into adulthood?

Grandparent benefits

Of course, relationships work both ways. Most grandparents find that their lives are enriched by their grandchildren. Below are some of the joys and gains that grandparents have identified.

Some joys of grandparenting

'Spending time with them and having more time now that I am retired.'

'Going to the pantomime with them and seeing their responses to the performance.'

'Being part of it all — at the school nativity, choosing books at the library.'

'Taking them out and doing things with them.'

'Spending Christmas together.'

'Seeing them growing up with their family and enjoying their pleasures.'

'Talking, playing and reading stories.'

'The children's acceptance of me and their love.'

'It's a great joy watching them develop and having the opportunity of doing things together.'

Some of the gains from being a grandparent

'Learning what is important to their generation.'

'The bond of love.'

'A new lease of life.'

'They've enriched our lives.'

And from the Mothers' Union study referred to earlier:

'We learn so much from their innocence, freshness and unstinting love — the house is young again.'

Some harder aspects of grandparenting

Having grandchildren is, on the whole, a welcome and positive experience for today's grandparents but it would be remiss of me to omit to say that some aspects of being a modern grandparent are hard as these quotations suggest:

'Because of the distance between our homes it is hard knowing that other people are nearer and closer and can be "grandparents" to them.'

'I find it hard not to step in when discipline is different from what I might have used.'

'Not intervening between parents and grandchildren can be hard — although this is only rarely.'

'Tiredness — I have not got the energy I used to have and want to do more than I am able.'

'It is hard watching the marriage of my son and his wife break up and not knowing what the split is doing or will do to my granddaughter. I am desperate not to lose touch with her.'

And some worries or concerns

Living as we do in a fast-moving western culture with its shifting value systems, our grandchildren are growing up in a world that is hard to understand. Grandparents worry about this. They are concerned about their grandchildren's safety, their insecurity, their education, the influence of television, the media, the Internet and peer group pressure. Some are concerned that their grandchildren are growing up with little contact with the Church and others who share their (the grandparents') faith.

Take Ten

Having read the four paragraphs above, reflect on your grandparenting situation and place a tick alongside any of the quotations or points with which you agree. Once you have done that add any further points of your own.

* Now reflect on this chapter and write down six key words that you think describe today's grandparents.

* Find a recent photograph of yourself. Mount it on card. Underneath write your name with the words, 'Grandparent to...' and the names of your grandchildren. Around the sides and top write the key words that you selected to describe today's grandparents. Put the photograph in a place where you will see it regularly.

A grandparent's prayer

Lord,
Thank you for my grandchildren —
for the love and joy that they bring to us
and for the privilege of being involved in their
lives, even if it is sometimes from a distance.

There are over sixteen million of us in Britain
alone and most of us do our best for our
grandchildren — BUT — we do need your help and
guidance and wisdom because sometimes being a
grandparent is hard.

I pray for my fellow grandparents now and ask for
your blessing on them and their grandchildren as
they grow together.

The grandparent adventure

You become a grandparent and have the opportunity to form an emotional attachment with the latest member of your family. The birth of your grandchild has given you a new name (Grandma, Grandpa or whatever) and status. It is time to become active and to begin the grandparenting adventure. How do you do that?

Sometimes it takes a while to grow into the role. Your circumstances, the meaning that you give to the role and your perception of the task will influence how you grandparent. Before thinking about yourself, however, let's consider how others have described active grandparents. Here are some words and phrases that have been used[1].

1. **Living ancestors** who are able to communicate family history to the children and to provide links with the past so that they gain a sense of their roots.

2. **Role-models** whom children might copy or choose to follow in terms of life choices, career, beliefs, behaviour, family commitment.

3. **Mentors** or teachers who enable children to learn skills e.g. baking or gardening, and who motivate and inspire children to ask questions, to experiment and to think.

4. **Nurturers** who are able to support and care for children directly, or indirectly through the support of parents, so that they grow and learn.

5. **Playmates** with time to play and do 'the unimaginable', especially in the early years. Later the role may become that of a pal or friend.

6. **Sources of wisdom** who encourage a sense of awe and wonder and with whom the mysteries of life can be shared. They can be relied on and are often sources of fun.

7. **Heroes** who are people to look up to.

8. **Transmitters of values and beliefs** who, through their lifestyles and actions, communicate what is of value to them.

Of course no one is suggesting that you create a curriculum for your task as grandparent but seeing it from different angles can sometimes help. Increased awareness, and sensitivity to what children may learn through their relationship with you, can enable effective grandparenting. Much of your significance in their lives and the learning and growth that they derive from it will come through informal, quality relating but how you are with them and what you do, or do not do, will have an effect.

My attention was caught recently by the sound of young children giggling. They were showing an elder how to crawl through a play tunnel and were delighted when he followed them through it. So was he! He was pleased that he could still get through such an object but most of all he was thrilled because he was seeing the world afresh through children's eyes. Earlier they had played with dough and created their own mini-world with their models and imaginative stories that the elder helped them to create. Later I saw them observing an insect that had crawled from under a stone and he was helping them to count the number of legs and to work out how the insect managed to walk without tangling them up.

These were simple, everyday incidents. The elder was not working with a curriculum in mind or testing whether these young children would do well in a baseline assessment. He was simply being with them, enjoying their company and exploring the environment to hand. Without realizing it he was also being a playmate, a mentor, a source of wisdom, a nurturer and no doubt a bit of a hero as well. Implicitly he was saying, 'I enjoy being with you. You are interesting, valuable people.'

When grandparents are able to enter children's lives like this, and to share interests as they grow, children are more likely to grow up with healthy attitudes towards themselves and older people because their grandparents have been good role-models. They have been pictures of people who care, who help children to know that they have value, who are interested in others and in the wonders of the world.

The grandparent adventure

It is often without lots of words that some of the grandparent's most dearly held beliefs and attitudes are communicated.

John is about to become a parent himself. When asked to think about the inheritance that his grandparents had left him it was the things that money could not buy that he saw as important — the importance of family and friends and respect for elders were values that he appreciated. How were these values communicated? Largely through shared experiences like picking the beans in Grandad's garden with him and taking them together to the homes of older friends and relatives who lived alone or who were unable to grow vegetables themselves. On such visits there was always a treat, a drink or a chocolate biscuit, but the best bit was listening to the yarns that older people had to tell. They were fascinating people who were still interested in life, including that of a young boy who had picked beans with his Grandad.

Take Ten

* Consider the list above. Which of the aspects listed would you include in your understanding of the role of grandparents? Are there other words or phrases that you might include or find more helpful?

* Reflect on some experiences that you have had with grandchildren and identify times when you have taken on specific aspects of the role as described in this chapter.

* If you do not yet have experiences on which to draw, imagine some instances/activities/events that might give you opportunities to take on some aspects of the role described. Note them down.

Being a grandparent is a long-term task. Your grandparenting has to be accommodated into the rest of your life. In a sense you grow up with your grandchildren. They obviously mature through stages of babyhood, reach early milestones like learning to walk, starting Toddler Group and later going to school. They grow through mid-childhood and puberty into their teenage years and before you know it they are young adults. Through their years of rapid growth you, the grandparent, are changing too. Not only do you have the opportunity of a life enriched by the presence of the next-but-one generation but you are doing your own growing and you have your own life challenges to meet. You may start the grandparenting years in paid employment and fit your grandparenting around your work schedule while coping with the onset of the menopause. By the time your grandchildren are young adults you may have been retired for several years, taken up new interests and possibly admitted that you feel twinges of arthritis and are constantly discovering new joints. In other words, not only will being a grandparent change your life but your life will be changed by natural maturation and by expected as well as unexpected life events. Nevertheless throughout this period you have the opportunity of journeying with your grandchildren and their parents. If you are able to sustain your relationship in ways indicated above then your life, and theirs, is likely to be like a great adventure though not necessarily a trouble-free one.

My mother telephoned me shortly after her eldest grandson's eighteenth birthday. She talked generally before focusing on the news surrounding the birthday celebration that she had received by telephone. Then she said, 'I never thought I would be the grandparent of an adult. Imagine having a grandson who is old enough to vote, to marry, to pay taxes.'

'Does that bother you?' I asked. 'No,' she replied. 'It is just that I was hit with the thought that he is an adult and not a child any more. Yesterday I realized that I must guard against treating him like a child. We are both adults.' She was indeed growing up with her grandson and becoming more aware of herself as well as of him at this new stage of her grandparenting adventure. Their journey continued — two adults each facing new challenges in life but one with more experience. From her I learned the importance of being both self-aware and aware of the life stages of those being grandparented.

Take Ten

Check your self-awareness. Think about the question: 'Who am I now, at this stage of my life?'

* To help you to answer the question jot down as many sentences as you can that begin with the words 'I am'. The sentences can include your name, the roles that you have, interests, fears, phobias, beliefs, memberships, feelings, health issues, new challenges that you face — anything that helps you to build a comprehensive picture of who you are now, at this stage of your life.

* Consider what you have written. How do you respond to the 'you' that you see? What do you like or appreciate about yourself? What

might you want to adjust? What new discoveries have you made about yourself? In what ways has the exercise helped you to be more aware of who you are now?

Being aware of self can help us in the adventure of grandparenting. It helped my mother when she discovered that her mental image of herself was of a younger person relating to young grandchildren when in fact many years had passed by since she was in that situation. She had to accept that she was getting older and she realized that there was still much that was exciting and good about life in later years as it was shared with adult grandchildren.

What is it that you can best offer your grandchildren at this stage of your life? The answer is likely to be what it has always been — a relationship based on love and commitment to the child or young person. As you move through life the detail of how you will relate, what you do together, what you share, and the frequency of visits will no doubt change. Sensitivity to, and the appropriateness of, changes in you, your grandchildren and their family contexts will help you to sustain the relationship. You will relate differently. For instance the conversation you have with a toddler is likely to differ in style and content from that you have with a teenager or young adult.

Times and people change, making the adventure more interesting but the principles and values that undergird the relationship remain the same. There needs to be a bond, an emotional attachment between grandparent and grandchild that usually occurs early in the life of the grandchild. It is a kind of falling in love that comes as the two interact in the early days. At this time the grandparent also needs to become aware of self as grandparent, to take on the identity of grandparent and to act like one. Grandparents who live at a distance may visit or spend time soon after the birth supporting parents and getting to know the baby. On returning home some of them may find the separation from their child and grandchild difficult. Chapter 11 explores some ways of grandparenting creatively from a distance.

The bonding with grandchildren experience enables grandparents to relive some of the emotions experienced when they first became parents themselves and it brings with it a range of other emotions as the family is changed by the addition of a new member. For many grandparents it is like having a second chance, an opportunity to learn from the past and to be a wiser person, sharing life with children with the benefit of hindsight. Even so the context of this second chance will be different from when they first parented. In 1970 the researcher Benedek stated,

'Thus grandparenthood can help the individual to integrate an altered body and self-image in at least two ways:
1) by identifying with their children, grandparents relive and rework their own parenthood as they observe their grandchildren's growth
and 2) by experiencing the grandchildren's love for and need for them, they obtain a new lease on life'.[2]

Take Ten

Reflect on your experiences of being a parent. Given a second chance, how would you parent differently? What have you learned from your experiences as a parent that you have taken or will take into your grandparenting adventure?

The grandparent/grandchild relationship has been described as special — perhaps that is a weak word for such a powerful and significant relationship. Some would say that there is no other relationship like it. One person expressed it this way: 'I have the fun and pleasure of having grandchildren and few of the hassles and responsibilities of being their parent.' It is true that most grandparents are not responsible for their grandchildren for twenty-four hours a day as they were for their own children. The burdens of parenthood are lifted from them and they are free to have more fun, to set aside part of their own agendas and to have more time for the children. Arthur Kornhaber suggests that this is a major reason why so many grandchildren experience the love of grandparents as unconditional[1]. If this is so, then grandparents have a vital role in enabling their grandchildren to glimpse, through experience, what is meant by the statement: 'God loves you'. God's love is completely unconditional.

There are some advantages in being one generation removed from grandchildren. It allows the relationship to be less complex than that of parent and child. This is because grandchildren do not usually need to separate psychologically and emotionally from grandparents in the way that they do with parents. Part of the normal process of growing up is to let go of some aspects of the intense relationship with parents, to become less dependent on them and more responsible for self. In the teenage years this is often evidenced by rows and power struggles between children and parents as they struggle with the process of separation. They have to learn to be individuals with a more equal relationship so that one is not primarily the giver and the other the receiver in the dependency stakes. It seems that in most cases children's attachments to grandparents continue through teenage and into adulthood because issues of dependency and authority are not present in the relationship. The grandparents' role, while being supportive, is different from that of parents. The generation gap allows grandparents to benefit from experience and to be more relaxed in the relationship.

One young person expressed her experience this way: 'My Nan is much more laid back than Mum', while a young mother explained:

'I think grandparents shouldn't have to "parent". They are allowed to spoil children and their unconditional love is part of the big picture for a young child and different from the "shaping" role parents have. For me grandparents are about enjoyment and fun although I would expect certain limits to be set... I think my views are influenced by the fact that my own grandparents had a similarly unconditional relationship with me. I was devoted to them and cannot remember any conflict. That is a very powerful memory and one I would like my children to share.'

So there is the real challenge of the grandparenting adventure — to relate to and love your grandchildren in such a way that they experience you as someone who loves them unconditionally, recognizing that through their experience of you they will learn and draw their own conclusions.

As **living ancestors** it is possible to give grandchildren a link with the past and help them to feel secure with roots in both the past and the present.

As **role-models** grandparents influence the choices they make and the values by which they choose to live their lives. Grandparents might even show them how to age with dignity.

As **mentors** grandparents might stimulate their imaginations and help them to learn skills for living, usually without much effort because they seem to learn from us through a mysterious form of 'osmosis'.

As **nurturers** grandparents can be part of an extended caring and support system that enables them to grow safely and healthily.

As **playmates** grandparents can have loads of fun, indulge their grandchildren and explore some of the wonders of the world. This is the role that perhaps gives the greatest pleasure but it can sometimes get grandparents into trouble with parents if they are perceived as overly spoiling their grandchildren.

As **sources of wisdom** grandparents can share stories, observe, explore and make discoveries with children that result in responses of awe and wonder.

As **heroes** grandparents can be trusted confidants whom children admire and to whom they can entrust their secrets.

As **transmitters of values and beliefs** grandparents can show children what their faith means to them and its consequent impact on their lifestyles.

Put like that, in terms of task, it may sound daunting. However, let's remember that what the grandchildren are looking for can be summed up quite simply. They want a person, a nan or grandma, a grandad, grandpa or elder who will love them, relate to them and share the journey of life. When grandparents do respond and take the opportunity to develop a loving and meaningful relationship with grandchildren they are likely to find that they have embarked on an adventurous journey of great significance. Many people who have already done so testify to the fact — and they also say that they received more from their grandchildren than they ever gave to them.

'Grandad showed me how to blink my eyes'

A grandparent's prayer

Lord,
Thank you for my grandchildren and for the
adventure of grandparenting to which you call me.

Help me to:

Affirm them.
Dialogue with them.
Value them.
Educate as I go.
Nurture and support them.
Travel alongside them.
Understand them.
Relate well with them.
Empathize with them.
Respond to their questions, joys and fears
and, above all, to their love.

May they experience their relationship with me as
unconditional and feel secure and loved in
consequence.

References

1 Kornhaber A, *Contemporary grandparenting* (SAGE Publications 1996), pp 88f, 74.
2 Benedek T, *Parenthood: Its Psychology and Pathology* (Boston: Little, Brown 1970), p 200.

Section 2: Grandchildren in context

Grandchildren in families

Mike and Pat's family

Mike and Pat Johnston planned to mark their wedding anniversary. After all it was an achievement to have stayed together for forty years, to bring up three children and now to be the grandparents of five. When they married, in the late fifties, they felt that they were making their vows for life, and meant it, but then forty years was a world away. They were fortunate. A few of their friends had not made it to this milestone, friends who also felt that marriage is for life but who, for various reasons, had not made it last that long.

When Pat was young the social event of the week was at the church youth club. That is where she met Mike. He left school at sixteen having done well in his exams. He learned a trade and achieved qualifications through a combination of day release and evening courses and worked his way up through his company. She did well at school and joined an accountancy firm in a secretarial role. When the children came along Pat did what most of her generation of mums did and that was to cease working for money and concentrate on parenting and home-making. When the children were all at school she returned to part-time work and went full-time again once the youngest was at secondary school. Mike saw himself as chief breadwinner and provider. He and Pat understood their roles though there had been tensions when Pat returned to full-time work. It had not been an easy time, but her return to full-time employment had helped to pay the mortgage. That was a long time ago and now they belonged to one of the most common forms of family in Britain, a three-generation family living in different households.

Anne's family

Anne, their eldest child, was thirty-seven. Like them her Christian faith meant a lot to her. After university and teaching she married David Foster, another teacher, and for a while they taught in a Christian school in Africa. During that time they presented Pat and Mike with two grandchildren, Amy and Emma. In those days telephone contact and travel were not so easy, making grandparenting from a distance hard. Pat and Mike had visited, with the financial support and encouragement of their own parents. They had learned the art of letter writing and in some ways shared in more depth through writing than some people do when they have regular face-to-face contact. Photographs, slides and cine-film had featured highly in their lives. Before Amy and Emma reached their teenage years the family returned to England and settled into a simple lifestyle, living in a semi-detached house a couple of hours' drive away.

Amy liked music, at least that is what she called it, and was popular with her peers, including the boys. Emma was the tomboy whose major crush was on the horses at the stables where she took riding lessons. Of course, having teachers for parents meant that Amy and Emma had their parents at home in school holidays and their work patterns, though difficult with all the changes in education in recent years, were similar to the children's school and study patterns. This meant that they were usually available for their children when needed. The values of the home were similar to those held by Pat and Mike. Family mealtimes were important and they were all still linked to a local church. It was easy to feel close and share in the life of the household even from a distance. At present Pat felt that Anne and David were struggling with the girls. They were growing up fast and showing signs of wanting to do 'their thing' rather than join in the family activities that they had previously enjoyed. Anne and David were going to have to 'let them go' eventually and that was one of the hardest things Pat had found that she had to do as a parent herself, especially when Anne and David had suggested going to Africa to work.

Bob's family

Bob, their second child, was thirty-five. After completing his computer science degree he joined a firm and did well financially. The work was demanding and the hours long. It seemed that Bob was driven by his work and had slipped away from church attendance. His parents had wondered if he would ever find the time to form a relationship and 'settle down'. They were surprised when, at the age of thirty-two, Bob introduced them to Ishbel, a colleague with a six-year-old son who had separated from her previous partner and was waiting for her decree absolute. At that time Bob and Ishbel, who was a Scot by birth, did not share much with Pat and Mike, simply that, once it was possible, they were to be married. Within six months they were married at the local Registrar's Office and set up home with Jamie, Ishbel's son, about twenty minutes' drive from Mike and Pat. Their home was at the 'posh end' of town and they lived a lavish lifestyle compared with the other households in the family. A year after their marriage they had a child, a girl called Chloe who was half-sister to Jamie. Ishbel returned to work as soon as her maternity leave was over — Pat and Mike hoped that she might opt for part-time employment but that had not been an option in the firm for which she worked. So, Jamie their step-grandchild and Chloe their granddaughter were added to Mike and Pat's number of grandchildren. Their child care was provided by a childminder and because they lived close to Pat and Mike they were able to see them most weeks.

Although the pressures of business were great, Bob made a priority of going to the home football matches with Jamie on alternate Saturdays or watching a match on television with him. Last Saturday Mike had joined them and they had a great time while Pat and Ishbel took Chloe to the park. She was pleased to have the opportunity of spending time with Ishbel — they had never been close but Chloe seemed to have brought them closer together. Ishbel had even asked for some advice on Saturday. Pat was glad that she had waited to be asked. There had been times when she wanted to say something about how Bob and Ishbel were bringing up the children but she bit her tongue. She felt that the childminder saw and knew the children better than Bob and Ishbel who only ate with them at weekends (alternate weekends for Jamie) because of their work hours, though they did ensure that they had a good holiday together each year. This pattern of parenting was so different from Pat's experience. In fact there was no such thing as parenting in her day when mums were mums and dads were dads. Each knew their role but now there seemed to be some confusion about roles and dads were not necessarily the main breadwinners and providers.

Charlie's family

Charlie was the youngest of Mike and Pat's children. Born some time after the other two, she was twenty-six and had a four-year-old child, Matthew. She lived in a small council flat furnished with second-hand furniture that she had been given. Officially she was poor in monetary terms but she would have been poorer still if she did not live near Pat and Mike, who provided child care for Matthew while Charlie worked part-time at the local hospital as a nursing assistant and studied for her OU degree. As a teenager Charlie had rebelled and been quite hard to handle. One of the most hurtful things she had said at the time was that her parents' faith was rubbish and she wanted nothing to do with it. Eventually she had gone to university but dropped out after eighteen months, having moved in with her boyfriend and taken a job at Pizza Hut. Her boyfriend had completed his course and started up his career ladder. The two had continued to cohabit. When Charlie became pregnant her partner felt that he was not ready to be a father and wanted her to have an abortion. Charlie knew that she could never go through with that and had hoped that they would marry. Instead they separated and Charlie came home to Pat and Mike who did all they could to support her.

There were times when Pat wanted to suggest to Charlie that she handle Matthew differently. She felt that he could wind his mother around his little finger, especially at bedtime when he would apply every trick in the book to delay the moment of going to sleep. Personally she had read one story and prayed with her children before bedtime. It had been an intimate time when they would share some of the happenings of the day and end with a goodnight kiss as she tucked the children up for the night.

Mike had always popped upstairs for a goodnight kiss too and on occasions he had supervised the bedtime routine, especially on the evenings when she went out to her mid-week group. For Matthew there was no real bedtime and very little structure except when he was in Pat and Mike's care. Then he seemed to adjust and accept their ways of doing things — like sitting at the table for meals and not in front of the television. Charlie had a *laissez-faire* style of parenting, as she had to life in general, but deep down she had experienced severe rejection when she and her boyfriend had separated. Pat admired the way Charlie had determinedly set about rebuilding her life and providing for Matthew. Although she had distanced herself from church when a teenager she had Matthew baptized in the local church shortly after he was born. That had surprised a few people!

Family diversity

Pat thought of her three children and the different families they had created — a nuclear family, a lone-parent family and a reconstituted or blended family. Each family was so different, not only in shape but in how it functioned. Between them they had presented Mike and Pat with four grandchildren and one step-grandchild whose names were definitely on the invitation list to the Ruby Wedding celebration. They were:

* Amy aged fourteen

* Emma aged twelve

* Jamie aged nine

* Matthew aged four

* Chloe aged eighteen months

Take Ten

Consider the three families of Mike and Pat's children.

* Draw them, using pin-people figures. Write under each one the type/shape of the family, e.g. lone-parent family. Note down some ways in which these families differ and some ways in which they are similar.

* Under each family type write some factors that affect how the family functions or works, e.g. patterns of employment, financial commitments, time together/apart.

* What are the basic values and beliefs that seem to affect how the people in the families live their lives?

* Now think of Pat and Mike. In what ways may the different family structures, values, beliefs and ways of living affect how Mike and Pat might grandparent their individual grandchildren?

* What do you think of Mike and Pat's policy of waiting to be asked before offering advice?

Families now

It may be obvious but your grandchildren live in families in which your children are the parents. The family life that your children create will in part be influenced by how you parented them, so will the way in which they care for and parent their children. Of course, past experience of you is not the only factor. While they may choose to follow your example, or ignore it, your children will be influenced by a partner (present or absent), by their personalities, by their times, i.e. culture and context, the latest understandings of and fads in child care, and by their beliefs and values. However, one thing is sure: your children want to do their best for your grandchildren and so do you. Parents and grandparents are on the same side when it comes to wanting the best for grandchildren. You may have different views on what is best, but thereby hangs a tale and the stuff of future chapters.

It sometimes helps grandparents to try to understand the family, the most influential context which grandchildren experience in their formative years. Like many families today Pat and Mike's grandchildren belong to a three-generation extended family living in a number of family units or households that are geographically spread. The individual units reflect much of what is happening in western societies where the most traditional of families is one where both parents have a job[1] and prefer to have two children rather than an 'only child'[2]. Some people choose to have no children and increasing numbers are unable to conceive a child. Families tend to be smaller than in years gone by and are often 'private affairs', isolated from other family and networks of support for a number of reasons such as cultural conditioning, family-unfriendly work patterns, house and estate design, and inadequate public transport.

While most babies are born to married couples, a major shift towards the early return to full-time employment of the mother has occurred in recent years[1]. As we saw earlier, Ishbel did not take a career break when she had Chloe, but a generation ago she probably would have done so. In 1992 almost one in two mothers returned to work before their child's fifth birthday[1]. The climate has changed and there is a host of reasons why mothers feel that they cannot leave the workplace. For instance, to purchase a home at current market values requires two salaries. As a result there is an increased need for child care. Many grandparents are able to supply this and in so doing support their children[3]. Pat and Mike are not unusual in caring for their grandson, Matthew, and in finding that he brings added value or meaning to their lives in retirement. However, not all grandparents live in circumstances where this is possible. They may be in employment themselves and/or caring for elderly relatives, or suffering from long-term illness, or have a range of other responsibilities, so it is important for grandparents to be realistic about how much and what form of support they can offer.

Like most people in their generation, both Anne and Bob had waited until their late twenties and early thirties before marrying. Charlie may choose never to marry. All three of Pat and Mike's children are in line with national trends, where we find that the average age for marriage is twenty-eight for men and twenty-six for women, and where there are increasing numbers of people choosing to stay single while being parents[2]. Of all births in England and Wales one third are outside marriage, so it is not unusual for people of Pat and Mike's generation to have a young grandchild who was born outside marriage. What is less usual is that Matthew's father did not stay in contact up to and beyond the birth of Matthew. Most babies born outside marriage are registered by both parents, who usually live at the same address, so the vast majority of children under five years of age do have both parents at home. (Sometimes bald statistics and sensational reporting can make the situation sound worse than it may be.)

It is now not uncommon to find cohabiting couples with children

In choosing to cohabit, Charlie was following the pattern of many of her peers. Church ministers often report that most couples coming to them for marriage are living together beforehand and, even if they are not doing so, they are usually sexually active. This includes young people brought up in the churches. Old patterns have been and are being questioned. Attitudes have changed. The only norm that seems to have been agreed is: 'If it is all right for me then it is all right. I do not necessarily expect the same to apply to you.' Self-fulfilment is the name of the game. Although most people hope and believe that their marriages will last we know that, should the divorce rate continue to rise, forty out of every one hundred of those marriages contracted in recent years will end in divorce[2]. To her cost Charlie discovered that her partner, Matthew's father, could or would not commit himself to marriage once she was pregnant. It used to be that the pattern for cohabiting couples was that they would marry if a planned or unplanned child was on the way. This pattern has changed in the 1990's. It is now not uncommon to find cohabiting couples with children, or increasing numbers of women choosing to keep a child and to parent alone —

unlike Charlie, it may be the woman who does not wish to marry. However, it is worth remembering that the vast majority of children under five are with both parents, married or unmarried, though the number of lone parents is increasing (about one fifth of all families with children in them) and Britain has the highest rate of teenage pregnancies in Europe.

While there are many children like Matthew living in a lone-parent family their reasons for living in such a family vary. Their parents may have married and been widowed or gone through a divorce. This was Jamie's situation for a short while before Bob married Ishbel and he gained 'an extra dad'. Seven out of ten divorcing couples have children. The vast majority of these children remain with their mothers but the numbers of children living with their fathers are increasing and there seems to be greater recognition of the influence that the fathering role might have on children, especially sons — but more of that later.

Like many children of divorced parents Jamie soon found himself moving from a lone-parent family into a stepfamily when his mother, Ishbel, married Bob Johnston. Around seven per cent of families with dependent children are step-families. In the United Kingdom, that included 800 000 stepchildren, like Jamie, in 1991 and a further 300 000 children born to both parents, like Chloe[3]. Of the stepchildren, three out of four have come from the woman's previous relationship and, if current trends continue, one in eighteen children is likely to become part of a married couple stepfamily before their sixteenth birthday[1]. This means that many grandparents, like Pat and Mike, can expect to acquire step-grandchildren like Jamie, when one of their children marries, remarries or takes a new partner.

The trends in family life quoted above are national trends that give some indication of what is happening to families in which many children live. Families too are unique and no family will fit the general trends exactly. It may be that you belong to an ethnic minority group and as you read this you are thinking that the picture painted hardly reflects the family life and structure that your grandchildren experience. It is true that patterns within ethnic minority groups, that include three million people in Britain, differ from those of the majority White British groups. For instance, among the Asian communities in Britain marriage figures are higher and divorce figures lower than those of the general population, while Black Caribbean and Black Other families are more familiar with cohabitation (13.7%) than the rest of the population (7.5%)[1]. There are historical and cultural influences that affect these living patterns that need to be considered before making any comparisons with the wider situation in Britain.

Take Ten

Every family is unique. Pat and Mike's grandchildren live in families that are diverse — with different forms and different ways of functioning. In some ways they each reflect national trends.

Think of your grandchildren and the families they live in, or will live in if you are to become a grandparent. Use a separate sheet of paper for each family unit and draw the families, using pin figures. Write the ages of the people alongside the appropriate figures.

Under each drawing write the type/shape of the family, e.g. nuclear, and jot down how the family unit reflects some of the trends described above. Jot down any unique qualities about each family.

As you consider each family, identify the good things that you see there and note them down, e.g. regular quality time spent by a parent with a child, laughter, members of the family who listen to each other, sharing of toys/possessions.

If you are the sort of person who likes to pray, use this information to formulate a prayer of thanks for the families in which your grandchildren live.

Keep this information for future reference.

Prayer

Lord, I bring to you the families to which my grandchildren belong.

May they fulfil their purpose in providing each child with a place of acceptance, so that all may grow knowing themselves loved.

References

1   Kiernan K, Wicks M, *Family and Change and Future Policy* (Family Policy Studies Centre/Joseph Rowntree Foundation, 1990)

2   Office of Population Census,1991

3   Joshi H, Davies H, Land H, *The Tale of Mrs Typical* (Family Policy Studies Centre, 1996)

Family milestones

When we consider the three family units in which Pat and Mike's grandchildren live, we see that there is something to affirm in each one. For instance: Anne and David Foster have always made time to chat with their children and do things together. Bob shares an interest in football with his stepson Jamie and they spend regular quality time watching matches and chatting about them. Charlie's love for Matthew is reflected in her determination to obtain her degree and provide for him. In most, if not all, family units there are some things that are positive and praiseworthy. It is also true that all will have a range of challenges to face or transitions to make. Let me explain further.

Many of these challenges to change will be normal and natural to families at the same stage of family life. Individuals reach milestones that affect the whole family. For example: the baby learns to crawl and climb, so new issues of safety have to be addressed such as the introduction of stair gates which the rest of the family have to negotiate. Most families at the stage of having toddlers in them will address similar safety issues and have to adjust to having mobile children within them. Families with young children in them will have their own normal, natural milestones, and so will those families where the children have reached the teenage years. Take Anne and David Foster with Amy and Emma. Theirs is what is known as an adolescent family. Parents in adolescent families, like Anne and David, have to become more flexible about family boundaries/rules in order to make it possible for their children, in this case Amy and Emma, to gain greater independence as they grow through their early teenage years. To enable this to happen parents and young teenagers need to agree new rules and to make adjustments in their relationships. It may be that the teenagers take more responsibility for themselves and the parents trust them to do so. Examples of rules or boundaries to be negotiated might include bedtimes, study times, use of telephone, pocket money, part-time work, and responsibilities within the household so that the youngsters can learn to take more responsibility and to come and go from the home. The challenges to adjust boundaries or rules and relationships are likely to be similar for most two-generation families containing young teenagers. At this stage the family is also affected by the challenges to parents when faced with the realization that their offspring will be fleeing the nest in the not-too-distant future and they must adjust to being a pair again. We can expect parents of young teenagers to be handling these issues and the teenagers themselves to be pushing for more autonomy. Sometimes life at home may feel uncomfortable but it is natural and normal!

Grandparents have already been through this stage or period of family life with their own children, now parents, so they may have some useful insights to pass on. Being available and approachable to listen to either parents or young people is an important role. Should this happen it is important that the listener-grandparents keep confidences and are non-judgemental. Sometimes reassurance that this is 'normal' to families at this stage is all that is needed. It is a great help to parents and young people to know that they are not the only ones handling such issues.

In addition to the natural milestones and challenges that Anne and David's family have come through to reach the adolescent stage, there have been other obvious transitions that are unique to them. They chose to work in Africa and returned home years later to work in an education system that had changed immensely during their absence. Amy and Emma no doubt had to make enormous adjustments when their parents chose to return to England and to settle into a culture and climate that was outside the girls' experience. Fortunately they came home to grandparents whom they knew and loved and that helped a lot.

Like their older sister Anne, Charlie and Bob have normal and natural milestones to celebrate and challenges to face. They also have their own specific transitions to make. Beginning with the natural milestones we see that they are at a similar stage in their family lives. It is the stage known as childhood, or young family. Both have young children and have had to adjust to parenthood with all the challenges that that brings. For both of them the extended family, especially their relationships with their own parents, Pat and Mike, have become more significant. This is often the case. During the late teenage years and young adulthood there is often a greater emotional distance between parents and their offspring, but once a grandchild is on the scene everyone moves up the generational ladder and relationships are changed. As one young mum said, 'I don't know how my mother did it. She brought four of us up and I'm exhausted with one.' Perhaps for the first time many young parents can really empathize with parents and appreciate (with some admiration) what they have done. Becoming first-time parents is recognized as one of the most significant and difficult transitions that have to be made in family life, i.e. when two become three. At this stage the new parents often draw closer to their own parents, now grandparents, valuing their support but not their interference. Of course, subsequent births require adjustments to the family system too and there are further mini-transitions to be made during the years of being a 'young family', such as when a child starts school. These are all change-points that are common to families with young children in them. I cannot emphasize enough that they are normal and natural challenges to family life but they may not always feel like it when you are living through them.

'We feel much closer to our parents now that we have a daughter ourselves'

For Bob and his wife Ishbel there are specific challenges to their family life that come from the fallout from Ishbel's previous marriage and the opportunities of building a new family. Bob and Ishbel set about forming their new family with all that that entailed while embracing a child, Jamie. Part of the challenge for Bob and Jamie was to form a step-parent/child relationship while a new marriage was being established and later to accept a new baby into the young family. As well as the normal transitions faced by a newly married couple and later by a family with a new baby, Bob's family faced added, complex challenges as they sought to become one family with children from two unions. These challenges are similar to those faced by others creating blended families with young children in them and may be said to be normal and natural to blended families, though each family may experience them and handle them differently. However, they are not transitions that have to be made by the majority of families of other shapes where there are young children.

Charlie and Matthew also face the normal challenges of being in a young family but the weight of the parenting role lies with one person instead of two. Having the practical and emotional support of Matthew's grandparents has eased Charlie's situation by allowing her to work and study while providing child care with adults who love Matthew and are significant in his life. Low income, often resulting in poverty, and the arrangements for access or non-access by the absent parent add to the complexities of family life and affect how expected milestones are handled.

It is natural for families to meet challenges and for family members to make adjustments in their relationships and ways of living together. If grandparents and others can provide encouragement and a bit of practical help they can sometimes support a family through a transition and prevent what is normal from becoming a crisis. Fortunately most families do manage to do this, often with the support of grandparents who may not always recognize the significance of what they are doing in preventing what is normal from becoming a crisis.

Let's remember then that all families are continually facing change because it is natural to do so. However, there will be some unexpected transitions that are thrust upon them, like those resulting from an accident or loss of work, and others which come from the choices that they make, such as the number of children they have (a choice for seven out of eight couples). Here it is worth noting that choices made by adults will affect the whole family including grandparents.

I like to think of families as giant mobiles. They twist and turn in the wind. Most of the time they are beautiful and, like moving works of art, they work well, or well enough. Sometimes, however, the wind pressure is too great for them and the strings of the mobile get tangled up. Often the tangles can be handled and the strings straightened out again so that the mobile more or less resembles its former self, if perhaps a little battered. There are other times, however, when the strings become so knotted up that they are beyond untangling and have to be cut in order to release the rest of the mobile. It helps if those of us wanting to support are aware of the natural challenges, i.e. the expected tangles in the mobile, that most families face when they have children in them. Here I am thinking of the natural milestones and challenges that the family might expect to meet at its stage of family life.

Take Ten

Think of the families to which your grandchildren belong and describe the stage of each family. Use the notes below to help you. You may find that a family straddles several stages. Life is not neat!

1. A family that is accepting new members into it, usually babies or young stepchildren, and in which young children live. The grandchildren in this family are likely to range in age from a few months to five years and child care may well be an issue.

2. A family with school-age children in it. Your grandchildren in such a family will be aged five to eleven.

3. A family with young teenagers in it. The parents are possibly beginning to refocus on their own relationship, or facing their own mid-life challenges and career issues while the children handle puberty and their search for identity.

4. A family that contains older teenagers who, over a number of years, are preparing to leave home. Your grandchildren in such a family are likely to be sixteen to twenty years old.

5. Young adults who are looking for partners, or choosing singleness and forming their own family units while adjusting relationships with their own parents and extended family. Your grandchildren in this family are likely to be twenty to thirty-plus years old.

6. Back to the family with young children in it but this time the children are your great-grandchildren! Wow!

What are the natural challenges or milestones (big and small) that your grandchildren's families can expect to meet at these stages of their family lives?

Record your thoughts on the family information sheets that you began in the previous *Take Ten* spot.

At each stage of family life both the adults and the children have a bit of growing up to do. We call it the developmental task. Probably the best thing a grandparent can do is to support when asked or needed, sometimes practically but often in a listening role rather than by giving answers — even if it is through a telephone conversation. Some family therapists suggest that major transitions may helpfully be marked with a celebration, a service, a ritual or a symbol.

Are there any opportunities in the near future for your grandchildren and their families to mark or celebrate some natural transitions in their family lives? Think of a way of marking the transitions or milestones yourself. Perhaps design a card to send or remember to make contact and mark it in your conversation.

In the Christian tradition churches offer services such as infant baptism or dedication, wedding ceremonies, confirmation or adult baptism and other celebrations that help to meet the whole family's, and sometimes the whole congregation's, need to mark a transition. For example: a wedding provides an opportunity for all present to mark the transition that the bride and groom are making and to see that there are implications for them, the guests. The parents of the bride and groom become in-laws and are helped, along with everyone else, to recognize that their children have completed the stage of leaving them in order to form their own unit. Other faith and non-faith groups have their equivalent ceremonies too.

At this stage note down any other changes or challenges that affect the families of your grandchildren at present, e.g. a loss or death, employment change, or the blending of two households. In subsequent chapters we will look at some of these challenges to your children's and grandchildren's family lives and consider what you might do.

Prayer

Lord,

Please help me to see milestones and challenges to family life as opportunities for the whole family to grow and change. Grant me wisdom to know when and how to offer support to my children and grandchildren and to do my part in helping them through difficult times.

Grandchildren in lone-parent families

When Charlie Johnston returned home to break the news that she was pregnant and going to be a single mother, her emotions were in a turmoil. Chief among them was a feeling of rejection. Her partner no longer wanted her if she had a child, but her principles did not allow her to have an abortion and anyway she wanted the baby. The most natural people to turn to were her parents, though not without a struggle. She knew that she had sometimes hurt them during her years of teenage rebellion and that her cohabiting lifestyle had not been in line with the beliefs that they held so dear. Deep down though, she realized that no matter what happened they loved her. They would identify with her pain and they would want the best for her child, their grandchild. One of the quotations that she associated with her mother was, 'There, but for the grace of God, go I.' Her parents were practical, empathetic people and it was practical support that she needed as she nursed her bruised ego and prepared for the birth of her child.

On hearing Charlie's news Pat and Mike Johnston felt sick, angry with Charlie's former partner and relieved that she had left him. They recognized their daughter's courage in coming to tell them her news and in choosing to leave her lover and keep the child. In their dreams they had always imagined Charlie happily married and presenting them with grandchildren but the real world is not like that. 'We can't change the past,' said Mike to Pat, 'but we can do something about the future.' And they did. They had seven or eight months to prepare with Charlie for Matthew's arrival. Matthew received a warm welcome into the world. His maternal grandparents, as well as his mother, were delighted with him. Then began their task of grandparenting a child from a lone-parent family. Were there ways in which it would be any different from grandparenting children from other types of family?

Pat and Mike were fortunate because Matthew lived nearby and they were able to spend regular time with him and supporting Charlie practically, financially and emotionally. They had to remember to respect the boundaries. Charlie was Matthew's mum and they recognized that they must try to co-operate with her in caring for Matthew. It was not always easy because they might have done some things differently but they found that it was best to talk things through with Charlie who, you remember, had been their volatile and awkward teenage daughter. Sometimes they resented what felt like 'being taken for granted', especially when it came to baby-sitting. Sometimes they were anxious about Matthew's future, especially when he started asking questions about his dad. At some point they knew that he would have to handle the feelings of rejection that come with the discovery that one of your parents did not want to know you when you were born. Or when he wanted to find his dad, perhaps to meet him. That, of course, may be a problem in the future. Meanwhile their important task was to be significant in Matthew's life, to be there for him and to enable him to grow up feeling as secure as possible. In doing that they must not step on Charlie's toes. Part of the route to supporting Matthew was in providing his mum with necessary back-up and that they did to the best of their ability.

There were times when Pat wondered about Matthew's other grandparents. Did they know of his existence? If they did, how would they feel about not having access to their grandson? It was something that just had not happened. As far as Charlie knew, Matthew's father had not told his parents, who were separated, and she did not have their addresses. Anyway she had wanted to make a complete break with Matthew's father, and for her that meant his parents too. Pat and Mike understood her attitude and hoped that Matthew would handle the situation as he grew and understood more. They believed that they should support Charlie while encouraging her to be honest with Matthew as he grew and asked questions.

Grandchildren find themselves in lone-parent families for a number of reasons. Some follow a pattern like Matthew's family; others may arise through the separation of a married or cohabiting couple or through the divorce of the parents. Some are the result of Britain's rising numbers of teenage pregnancies, while increasingly women in their twenties and thirties choose to have a child and to remain single. In a few families, less than seven per cent of all lone-parent families in the UK, the parent has been widowed. The experiences of living in a lone-parent family will vary partly because the reasons for lone-parenthood differ and so do the circumstances. For instance, the age at which an unmarried mother gives birth to a child might well affect her readiness to parent and her ability to provide for a child.

Louise and Lyn

Take two families. In one the mother, Louise, gave birth to a daughter, Ellie, at the age of seventeen. She left school with few qualifications and felt that she gained real significance when she had a child. With the support of her parents, the maternal grandparents, she cared for her baby and a close bond developed between them. The child, Ellie, flourished and, with the support of the local council and her parents, Louise created a home. Like many other lone parents she did a fine job with the resources available to her. When Louise was ready to find a job while her extended family provided child care she found that she could not earn enough to make it worthwhile. Lack of qualifications meant that she could only get a low-paid job and that she would be worse off financially because she would lose some of her benefits. Louise budgeted well but it was always a struggle to keep out of debt and that worried her. Like many in her situation Louise found that low employment prospects and lack of money caused pressure. Others in similar positions to Louise but without grandparent or other support, for whatever reason, find that the lack of good affordable child care adds to their pressures. Often the combined pressures that can lead to debt also lead to low self-esteem in parents and that in turn affects their children.

Lyn, the parent in the second family, had reached her mid-thirties when she began to worry that the biological clock would run out before she had a child. Her trouble was that she had not found anyone with whom she wanted to spend the rest of her life and have her children. She had focused on the career that she enjoyed immensely, and had bought a house. Most of her friends were associated with work and she had a series of short-term intimate relationships. When she became pregnant at the age of thirty-eight, she was pleased and so was the father, though they both realized that they would be better remaining friends than marrying each other. She wanted a child and would manage very well with the help of a child carer whom she could afford to pay and, if necessary, she would go freelance so that she could work from home and fit work around her child. The father would remain a friend and have access to the baby who would be brought up knowing his father. The tricky thing would be telling her parents that they were to be grandparents when there had been no wedding. It would be a shock for them. As Christians they might find it hard to accept her behaviour and to appreciate her joy at being pregnant.

Of course, her parents were shocked when she told them and silent for a while. Yes, they wanted to be grandparents but had never envisaged circumstances such as these. They needed some time to accept the situation, did not want to jeopardize their relationship with their daughter and wanted to find a way of telling their friends. Eventually they became proud and supportive grandparents, travelling a hundred miles from their home to visit Lyn and her son Harry regularly and to baby-sit at weekends when Lyn had to work.

The stories speak for themselves. In each of them the grandparents have opportunity to take an important role and to become significant people in the lives of their grandchildren as they grow and mature. However, not all grandparents would want to grasp the opportunity. Some may be unable to do so while others have their own plans for this stage of their lives. They may have limited time to give because they have jobs and may still be engaged in parenting their own younger children. Among the grandparents will be some who are lone parents themselves who are coping with living on a low income. And it may be that the grandparents' own children distance them, feeling that they must bring up their children alone. There are no blueprints for grandparents of children in a lone-parent or any other type of family, only guidelines.

Take Ten

* Take Charlie's, Louise's and Lyn's families in turn and imagine that you are the prospective grandparent. How would you feel on being told that you were to become a grandparent? How would you react initially and how do you think you would react on meeting the baby?

* Think of the three children — Matthew, Ellie and Harry — in their respective families. In what ways are their families similar? What factors are different about their families? What particular challenges do you think that they might meet in life because of their specific family circumstances?

* Imagine that you are Matthew's, Ellie's or Harry's grandparent. How might you contribute to their lives as they grow, and help to prepare them for some of life's challenges?

When separation and divorce occur

The chief reason that grandchildren live in lone-parent families is that their parents separate and, if married, divorce, for a range of reasons. Increasingly this is the experience of younger children as the average length of marriage decreases. As we all know, separation and divorce is a painful process for the adults involved, but what about the children? Few come through their parents' separation and divorce unscathed. I do not know any. How they respond depends partly on their age. Younger children feel without understanding. They sense that things are wrong and sometimes feel that it, whatever it is, must be their fault. Often their parents' responses to them change — stress causes them to be less tolerant, to be irritable, to snap, to withdraw. Parents may respond differently but children know that something is wrong and conclude that they are to blame. They know that Mummy or Daddy is sad because there are tears. They know that they are angry because there are harsh words and/or ominous silences.

When the time comes for them to be told that their parents are separating, the reactions of children depend partly on how they are told. It helps if both parents can be part of the communication process but there is no easy way of communicating such news to children. Many feel that their rock, the source of their sense of security, is crumbling beneath them. They want to know details about where they will live and need to know that the parent who is leaving still loves them. They will need this reassurance for a long time, perhaps always, and they will be helped if clear access arrangements are made so that they know when they will see the absent parent. Sadly many parents, especially fathers, lose contact with their children within the first two years after a divorce and a consequence of this is that some grandparents also lose contact with their grandchildren.

Children have feelings

Some people suggest that children are resilient and they will 'bounce back' but children have an emotional life as well as adults. Rather than assuming that they will do so, it is wiser to do what we can to enable them to make the necessary adjustments to their new circumstances and this is where grandparents can be of help. Of course, the degree to which they can help will vary. Sometimes emotions and family conflict might get in the way. Let's be honest. It is the grandparent's son or daughter who is going through the divorce and there will be feelings about that. Grandparents have their own emotions to deal with and may find it difficult to be neutral where their son- or daughter-in-law is concerned. If it is the son or daughter that is the leaving parent then how much access grandparents might have will depend largely on the closeness of their relationship with the custodial parent. Equally, a son or daughter may turn to their parents, the grandparents, for support during the times when the children come to stay in school holidays or at weekends. So we see that a separation or divorce can mean that grandparents have more opportunity to be with their grandchildren, but sometimes it means that they have fewer opportunities.

Grandparents who are able to remain in contact with their grandchildren can give them a sense of continuity. For children with a close relationship with grandparents there is often a sense of being known by the grandparents and of knowing them. After all, grandparents have always been there. They provide children with some roots and help them to feel safe when all around is changing. In 1990 A N Tetrick[1] found that a strong relationship with a grandparent is helpful to all children as they make emotional and social adjustments. This suggests that important bonding with grandchildren in the very early years places grandparents in a good position to support their grandchildren during the process of a divorce and beyond. Children seem to say, 'Be there for me in the hard times as well as the easy ones.' And being there means doing ordinary things with them, sometimes activities that help them to get rid of feelings — like washing the car with Grandad or Grandma, or using energy digging, or baking (especially pastry or bread), or mastering a new computer game. Sometimes it means helping financially, when possible, because divorce leaves people financially less well-off. It also means being non-judgemental, or not taking sides with one parent as far as the children are concerned — not always an easy thing to do!

Circumstances change

Maggie had a close relationship with her granddaughter Holly. Her son and his wife lived nearby and she spent lots of time with the youngster playing, visiting the park to feed the ducks, reading books and generally enjoying her company. There came a point when she noticed that Holly was becoming more withdrawn and eventually she learned from her son that he and his wife, with whom

Maggie had a good relationship, were not getting on. They argued a lot and their arguing was loud. It was affecting Holly and, although he had tried to persuade his wife that they should get help, she was reluctant. After a while he decided to move out of the marital home on a temporary basis to see if that would help the situation. He was thinking primarily of his daughter, who needed a calmer atmosphere, and he arranged to have her to stay most weekends. After several attempts to make the marriage work the couple decided that their best option was to separate permanently and to file for a divorce. The one thing that they could both agree on at the time was that they must work together as divorced people to do the best for their daughter.

Saddened by the circumstances Maggie also decided to do the best that she could for her grandchild and to support her son as he cared for her at weekends. Each weekend they spent some time with Maggie and the rest of her family. A close relationship was sustained between her granddaughter and herself. They did things together, just the two of them. Simple things like washing up, reading stories, painting, and gardening. Maggie's garden became a play haven for Holly and some of her school friends. As far as her granddaughter was concerned Maggie's home was a peaceful place. It was where Grandma was and Grandma always seemed to have time for her. Some years later, however, Maggie's access to Holly was not so easy — but more of that in the next chapter.

Older children and separation

Older children and young people are also affected when their parents decide to separate or divorce. Some people assume that the experience will not be so bad for them but in my experience that is not what they may think at the time. There is grief, a sense of loss sometimes tinged with relief at not having to live with constant argument or 'atmosphere' but there are great adjustments to make. Those who have enabled them to have a sense of security in the past have shifted the goal posts and, at least temporarily, some young people will feel unable to step out into their future as confidently as they might have done. Others withdraw as a form of self-protection while others show that they are hurting through their behaviour, which may change dramatically. Older children and young adults have to adjust their relationships, the running of the home is changed and young people react differently. Often the questions that come first are practical: 'Where will I live?' 'Can I keep my room?'

'Will we keep this house?' 'How will this affect me?' Sometimes there is denial, sometimes anger, sometimes disillusionment. Sometimes youngsters do not share with anyone what is happening to them at home. There can be a whole host of emotions swirling around and joining those raised by the pressures of important exams or decisions to be made about the young person's own future. Again grandparents who have a significant relationship with their grandchildren can be a huge support. They are still there, even though they might not understand fully. Sometimes young people who are growing away as a natural part of their development draw nearer again, at least for a time. One young person started to visit his grandparents at lunch-time during the school dinner hour. They enjoyed his company, one being housebound, and were probably unaware that at this time of upheaval in his life their grandson experienced them as stable and secure. While everything else in his life was changing they were not, and he was glad.

The grandparent-grandchild relationship can be very special. As has been said elsewhere, one of the strengths of the relationship is that grandparents are one generation removed from a lot of the issues faced by parents and their children. This is no more so than in the case of children in lone-parent families where the process of becoming 'lone-parent' can be painful and confusing. Sometimes the process can take several years but, for a few, becoming the child of a lone parent can happen instantly through an accident or illness. In the midst of such sadness grandparents can appear to be the calm ones. For many grandchildren, coming to their grandparents can be like coming from the rough ocean into the shelter of the harbour.

After the initial trauma of the separation and divorce of their parents, many children settle into a routine, often living in two homes, having two sets of toys, visiting maternal and paternal grandparents with their respective parents. As children grow, the patterns are adjusted. Again the role played by grandparents will be influenced by their relationship with their own son or daughter, by geography and accessibility, by personal circumstances, and grandparents have to work with the art of the possible. Most grandchildren value the friendship, love and any support that grandparents can give even when physical access is denied. Usually it is possible to telephone, to send birthday and Christmas presents and to keep channels of communication open with the children — but it requires persistence and sometimes tact when making arrangements with parents whose relationship is strained. Remember that former sons- and daughters-in-law sometimes feel awkward with grandparents, no matter how well-meaning they are. When grandchildren feel that they are special to you then they are likely to believe it and to feel better about themselves. Tough life experiences can damage confidence and self-esteem but warm and loving grandparents can help grandchildren to recognize the good news that they are loved and valuable people no matter what has happened in their family life.

Take Ten

* Imagine that a friend of yours has grandchildren whose parents are separating. S/he asks you how best s/he might support the children. They are a boy aged four and a girl aged nine and they live about ten minutes away by car. Make a list of general guidelines or advice that might be helpful.

* Consider your guidelines. Would you adjust them if it was your friend's son and daughter-in-law who were separating? If so, how? What further advice might you give if there was a teenager in the family?

A prayer for lone-parent families

Lord,

I bring to you those children who live in lone-parent families for whatever reason.

Grant to their grandparents the wisdom to know how best to support them and their parents — when to act and when to do nothing, when to speak and when to remain silent.Through their words and actions may their grandchildren and children know that they are loved.

Reference

1 Tetrick A N, 'The grandchild-grandparent bond' in *Dissertation Abstracts International*, 51(6), 3150B

Grandchildren in blending families

Three years after Holly's parents divorced, her mum found a new partner, whom Holly called by his first name though he would have liked her to call him Dad. She refused because she said she already had a dad. In the time that she had been alone with her mother they had developed a loving and close relationship, then her mother's new partner came on to the scene and Holly had to adjust. She took some reassuring that her mother loved her just as much as before but soon learned that there were some benefits to having another adult around. In this case, she had someone to encourage her with her computer skills during the week and stepbrothers and -sisters who visited in the holidays. At weekends she continued to be with her Dad and spent a lot of time with Maggie, her grandmother. Maggie was not the sort to pry, more of a listener, and occasionally when they were baking, or whatever, Holly would talk about the adjustments she was making at home. Sometimes she asked for advice but mostly having someone to talk to in the normal course of events was what Holly needed. She seemed to accept that mums and dads divorce and get new partners. Many of her friends had similar experiences.

Two years later and five years after his divorce Holly's father found a new partner whom Holly called by her first name. They worked hard at their relationship, taking it one step at a time. Holly gained more stepbrothers and -sisters. Her family was growing. During this period Maggie was consulted about how best to integrate Holly into the new family and she remained close to her grandchild. Through this period Maggie had to make her own adjustments. There was a sense of loss because her granddaughter was no longer with her every weekend. Holly's family had extended to include two sets of step-grandparents, aunts, uncles and cousins as well as stepbrothers and -sisters. Maggie had to share her granddaughter with more people. Her concern was to be there, should Holly need her, and to do what she could to ensure that she remained a secure child. Maggie also gained some step-grandchildren and began a whole new set of relationships as a step-grandparent.

From the outside Holly's family might have looked complicated but to her there was a sense of belonging to more people once she was used to her stepmum and had developed a relationship with her. Life does not stand still and in time Holly also accepted two half-sisters into her family when both her parents had babies with their new partners. However, her Gran-Maggie is still special and sometimes Holly will ask if she can come and stay while her stepbrothers and -sisters are visiting their birth-father, and sometimes she joins Maggie on family holidays when the step-grandchildren are with their paternal grandparents. One of her favourite activities is rummaging through her Gran's boxes of family photographs and hearing stories from the past, stories about her early childhood, her grandad who died and her great-grandparents who were part of her early childhood. Together Holly and her Gran-Maggie are making a family scrapbook and Holly asks about the different family and stepfamily relationships to explore how she, her half-sisters and her stepsiblings fit together in the family jigsaw.

Holly now belongs to two stepfamilies, her mum's and her dad's, but she sees them as two parts of her family. Sometimes stepfamilies are called blended families or reordered families, but because families are always changing they are constantly in a process of blending or reordering. No two stepfamilies are the same. When a stepfamily is formed some grandparents lose time with their grandchildren, some gain step-grandchildren, and others have to share their time between their grandchildren and step-grandchildren.

When Bob Johnston married Ishbel his parents, Pat and Mike, gained a daughter-in-law and a step-grandson, Jamie, at the same time. In two short years Jamie moved from being in a couple family with his birth-father and mother to being in a lone-parent family with his Mum, to being in a blended or reordered family with his stepfather, Bob. He had to handle so much change with the decisions about where and with whom he would live being made for him. As well as gaining a stepdad he gained a set of step-grandparents, some stepaunts, uncles and cousins. Like Holly he also had to accept a half-sister into his life. For children living in a stepfamily, like Jamie, family life requires a good deal of adjustment. There are pecking orders to sort out among the children, and parents' love is often tested too. Does s/he love me as much as his or her own children? Do they get more treats than I do when they visit their father while I stay at home with mine and his new partner? Who do I belong to now? Which weekend is Dad's and which is Mum's and is it Mum's or Dad's turn to have me for Christmas this year?

When a new stepfamily is formed some pain may be caused for grandparents who have bonded with their grandchildren but who find that they have less access to them. Indeed some may find that they lose contact and that is very sad. The children and their new family may move further away or relationships may be strained. In each case it is best if the adults concerned ask what is best for the child. After all children are not the possessions of parents or grandparents. If at all possible it is good to stay in touch and to do so with the consent of the parents. The grandparent/grandchild relationship is so special that it is worth working and negotiating for, and if a grandparent is well bonded with a grandchild it is likely that the child is going to want to keep in touch. Visits, holidays, time together have to be carefully planned because there are more people in the new family to consider. But they are important because grandparents with access to their grandchildren can continue to support them through times of change, to give a sense of continuity, to listen and encourage, to nurture and to play, to have fun and to laugh. They can continue to help their grandchildren to build good memories that will help them to feel secure as they grow. Some of these memories will be shared with step-grandchildren too.

Grandparents, of course, have feelings. They care for their grandchildren. At the time of the break up of their son or daughter's previous relationship they often become more active in their grandchildren's lives. When the new partner appears they may feel unsettled and wonder how their role will change. Some may panic about losing their grandchildren, especially if they are the parents of the non-custodial parent — they will always be a reminder of the ex-husband or ex-wife. If their son or daughter is the custodial parent and they continue to have a good relationship with the ex-partner then feelings are likely to develop that affect how the custodial parent feels about them. Often the new partner feels that the grandparents are watching to see how well he or she is doing with their grandchildren, and new partners sometimes perceive a sense of disapproval even when none is intended because they are themselves vulnerable in their new family situations. It may become particularly difficult when the grandparents find it hard to restrain themselves from suggesting what may be best for their grandchildren and step-grandchildren. Despite the difficulties, however, it is possible to be supportive of the new family unit. Writing about her own in-laws Brenda Maddox[1] said, 'They never interfered or even gave advice, but were always ready to help out and provide for my stepchildren and children alike a steady supply of love and home-made birthday cakes. And they appreciated me. "Granny says we should be nice to you," my stepdaughter informed me rather disgustedly when she was small. "She said that if it weren't for you, we'd be in a fix."'

In order to grandparent and step-grandparent well it is worth remembering the following:

1. It is helpful to be as aware as possible of your own feelings. Be honest with yourself. Once aware of your feelings you can avoid acting on feelings alone with the stepfamily and the children within it. Instead ask what is best for the children and act on your answers to that question.

2. Remember that in most stepfamilies there are three kinds of children, i.e. his, hers and theirs. Each will experience the new family differently so it is worth mentally stepping into their shoes to imagine family life from their point of view. Include in your thoughts how each child might perceive and experience you. Imagine what it might be like for any leaving or re-entering the family because they have had time out with a non custodial parent or another set of grandparents, perhaps for a holiday.

3. In stepfamilies there can be a lot of rivalry among the children. One cause of that rivalry can be how the children experience and perceive their grandparents and step-grandparents. Whose grandparents remember all the children's birthdays, i.e. their step-grandchildren and their grandchildren? Do they treat the children equally giving presents of roughly equal value? Do they do fun things with their step-grandchildren as well as their grandchildren? Do they give them all some individual attention?

4. It is wise to avoid indulging grandchildren with expensive gifts and treats that they do not need. It is not good for the children. The best gifts that can be given are time and love, even if the time is

by telephone or e-mail. Indulging step/grandchildren can sometimes cause parents to feel angry or helpless and it does not help parent-step/grandparent relationships.

5. Do not expect too much from step-grandchildren. They will need time to get to know you so do not be surprised if they are rather guarded with you or do not appear to appreciate your offers of love — at least in the early days. Persevere and try to be consistent.

6. Sometimes it helps for stepchildren to have a special name for step-grandparents such as Gran-Maggie. As the children accumulate more grandparents the special name helps them to differentiate between the members of the grandparent generation and as one stepmother said, the name Gran or Nan adds a note of respect for the older generation. She wanted her children and stepchildren to use more than a first name with their elders.

7. Remember that your son or daughter is an adult who has chosen the path of step-parenthood and possibly parenthood. Respect his or her decision.

8. As Brenda Maddox indicates, a little support and appreciation goes a long way so support without interfering and express sincere appreciation whenever you can.

And some points from the National Stepfamily Association:

* Like children, grandparents do not have much say in what happens and yet they may provide considerable support. Grandparents and step-grandparents can be advocates for their grandchildren — understanding challenging behaviour, helping them to understand decisions taken on their behalf by their parents and helping parents to see their children's viewpoint.

* Being a step-grandparent is not the same as being a grandparent — there is no biological connection. It takes time to develop affection, responsibility and loyalty. It is a complicated role and has to be negotiated with all other family members — the welfare of children should be the priority... Try to focus on the needs of all the children and to provide help that is wanted rather than what you want to give.

* Try to treat grandchildren and step-grandchildren the same, e.g. at birthdays. If in doubt about what to do, try to see things from the children's points of view. More complicated issues may arise over inheritance so it is important to make a will and to seek advice from a Family Lawyer. There is no automatic provision for

stepchildren or step-grandchildren. And what if you become ill or frail and require their support?

* If possible, keep in touch, especially through times of change. Do not think that stepfamily life will be easy or that it is second best. A stepfamily is a new family and offers the hope of new relationships and closeness for adults and children...

(From an information sheet published by The National Stepfamily Association.)

Take Ten

Suppose you are a friend of Gran-Maggie or Pat and Mike Johnston. You have received a letter explaining the family situation and asking for some help and advice about being a step-grandparent as well as a grandparent to children in the same family. Write a letter of encouragement and give advice that you think you would appreciate if you were in their shoes.

'I have lots of grandparents: Nanny Lizzie and Grandpa Felix, Nanny Janet and Grandpa Jim, Nanny Ann and Grandpa Frank, and Nanny Sue'

The prayer of grandparents in blending families

Lord,

From the outside they look so complicated and so BIG compared to some of the small families that we have become used to.
We call them blended families.

Please help us to encourage them in their blending...
by being sensitive to their particular circumstances and challenges;
by placing the needs of our grandchildren and their stepbrothers and sisters before our own feelings;
by encouraging our children and their partners in their parenting and step-parenting roles;
by being practical and just in our support;

and may we celebrate with them the opportunity that their family gives to us of creating a lively, dynamic extended family in which children and adults can learn and grow.

Reference

1   Maddox B, *Step-parenting* (Unwin Paperbacks 1975), p 147.

Parents and grandparents

Most parents go into parenthood with high hopes and even higher expectations of themselves as parents. Then comes the reality. Their bundle of joy arrives, they fall in love with him or her, but the responsibility is awesome and they are so tired. There are no days off. How will they manage? Is it possible for them to match up to the high hopes that they have and to the expectations that they perceive society placing on them? Certainly, parents do seem to get a bad press and many feel inadequate for the task. Consider the job description:

*'**Wanted**: A responsible person, male or female, to undertake a lifelong project. Candidates should be totally committed, willing to work up to twenty-four hours daily, including weekends during the initial sixteen-year period. Occasional holidays possible, but may be cancelled at no notice. Knowledge of health care, nutrition, psychology, child development, household management and the education system essential. Necessary skills: stress management and conflict resolution, negotiation and problem-solving, communication and listening, budgeting and time management, decision-making, ability to set boundaries and priorities as well as providing loving support. Necessary qualities: energy, tolerance, patience, good self-esteem, self-confidence and a sense of humour. No training or experience needed. No salary but very rewarding work for the right person.'*[1]

Could anyone match up to the description of the parental task described? As grandparents you have been there and got the T-shirt. You have parented and know the joys as well as the difficulties involved in bringing up children and you know that, basically, parenting is about loving, relating to and nurturing children as they grow and develop. Yes, it is an important, vital task but you do not have to have a distinction grade in all the knowledge, skills and qualities described — a pass will do and some of the passes might be obtained along the way. Most parents are good enough — by that I mean that their children grow up to be reasonably well-adjusted adults and take their place in society — and they will do even better if their parents are enabled to be more confident about their parenting.

Take Ten

Think about your own parenting years.

* ✳ What do you wish that you had known about parenting before you started?
* ✳ Which skills and qualities did you find you needed most?
* ✳ What sort of support did you value, if any, and where did it come from?
* ✳ How did you manage to get 'time out', an evening or weekend without the children — if at all?
* ✳ In what ways did you find parenting a rewarding task?

When Pat and Mike Johnston discussed the questions above they realized that they had been fortunate. Their own parents, the grandparents of Anne, Bob and Charlie, had lived nearby and enjoyed their role as grandparents. They liked taking the children out, having them at their homes, or babysitting while Pat and Mike went to the cinema. In fact, Pat and Mike had had more time to themselves than they realized. In addition they had been supported practically and financially when the grandparents, relatives and friends bought gifts of clothes and toys and treated them to the occasional holiday. Yes, they had been extremely fortunate parents who had been given time to nurture their own marriage relationship while in the parenting years. Many people did not have that opportunity.

What Pat and Mike had valued most, however, was the way in which the grandparents had assisted them. Both Pat and Mike had come from families in which it was normal to care and co-operate with each other and their parents had carried this over into the way in which they supported Pat and Mike as parents. There was a feeling of mutuality. Yes, the grandparents supported them but there were ways that Pat and Mike were able to help their parents, especially in some of their decision-making and in practical things like car maintenance.

Parents and grandparents

They would consult each other and there was an air of what Kornhaber[2] calls 'respectful co-operation'.

Having co-operative parents who cared meant that Pat and Mike had mentors. They certainly could not say that they had all the knowledge, skills and qualities described in the job description above when Anne was born, though they had some of them. They also had experience of working with children in their local church. Instead they had encouraging parents who enabled them to be confident in their parenting and who gave them wise advice when asked. Sometimes they even made suggestions that were unasked for but again their style, and quality of relationship, meant that what they said was considered and often accepted. Pat and Mike were grateful to their own parents for what they had shown them about parenting and they were thankful that Anne, Bob and Charlie had grandparents who were significant in their lives. They were also very proud of their three adult children and loved them dearly.

When their first grandchild, Amy, was born Pat and Mike were unable to be alongside their daughter Anne and her husband David in the ways that their own parents had been alongside them. Amy and, later, Emma were born in Africa and their parents faced the challenge of parenthood without many of the conveniences that people in Britain might take for granted. However, Pat and Mike did learn to be alongside and to co-operate in a way through letter-writing. Anne and David kept them in touch with the growth and development of their grandchildren, shared what they were picking up from African friends and mentors about parenting African-style and sometimes asked for help or advice. Similarly, Pat and Mike shared what was happening in their lives and asked for opinions and sometimes advice. Now that Anne and her family were back in Britain, Pat and Mike felt in a good place to support while Anne and David faced the challenges of parenting teenagers.

Through their earliest experiences of wanting to support Anne and to grandparent well, Pat and Mike realized that some of the lessons they had learned from their own parents would provide helpful principles. They were naturally caring and co-operative people. They would aim to co-operate with their adult children and to support them while recognizing that the contexts in which their children were parenting were different from the one in which they had brought up their children. To be helpful they needed to understand them.

Take Ten

Again think of your own parenting years.

* Consider your expectations, baby- and child-rearing practices that were encouraged, work patterns, home, schools, pressures on you as a parent, concerns for your children, your social activities, the role of the Church, how you spent family holidays and so on. In other words, build up a picture of the context in which you parented.

* Now do a similar exercise thinking of the contexts in which your children parent. How are they the same and how are they different?

Here are some of the points that Pat and Mike identified about parenting today.

* Work practices have changed. Some people have too much work and some too little but on the whole parents are ambitious to go up the professional ladder if they can. To do that requires time that may otherwise have been given to parenting. Some children hardly ever see their fathers in the week because they are working such long hours and are expected to do so by employers. Other fathers are at home too much because they cannot find a full-time job. Most mothers work, often part-time. Time out having a child adversely affects their career prospects because their field of work changes so rapidly. Mothers are returning to work when their children are a few months old. In addition no one has a job for life and so there is insecurity at work which affects the overall well-being of parents and children when there are financial commitments to undertake.

* Consumerism has affected people's expectations about what a home should be. Years ago people planned to gather furniture and build a home over the years. Now many expect to buy a home immediately and furnish it with essential items that would not have been dreamt of years ago. Consequently parents bringing up children live with extremely high mortgages and other debts.

* Parents travel long distances in the course of their work and are more mobile. Some commute to mainland Europe for the day. Such travel adds to the working day and reduces contact with children.

Parents and grandparents

* Many parents are juggling paid work, keeping the home going and parenting. They are very stressed as a result and always in a hurry. Stress and tiredness affect relationships and sometimes mean that parents are impatient with children. Hurried children can become stressed themselves.

* Child care provision is patchy and expensive. To put a child in the local nursery costs £140 a week, which is heavy on the pocket of parents but cheap at the price when you consider the importance of good child care.

* Parents who stay at home to care for their children often feel very isolated and lonely. They feel they should cope alone and are often unsupported. Depression is a problem for many young mothers.

* Feelings of guilt among parents seem to have reached epidemic proportions. So have low self-esteem and feelings of not being good enough. Many have extremely high expectations of themselves as parents and some of their guilt comes from not being able to reach those expectations.

* Parents fear for their children's safety and prefer them to stay at home playing on a computer than going out to play with friends. When they do go out their parents take them in the car — no time to walk — and arrange a time to pick them up again.

* With the implementation of the core curriculum and testing at specific ages in primary schools, parents and children feel pressurized and 'on trial'. This seems to have led to an undervaluing of play in some pre-schools and homes. Comments like 'You can play when you have finished your work' communicate to children that play is less important than literacy and number work, and that it is not part of the process of becoming literate and numerate.

* Parents are bringing up children in a more multi-cultural and pluralistic society. There is a greater diversity of people, backgrounds and faiths.

* The influence of the media for good and ill is powerful with more children having their own computers and televisions in their bedrooms so that they spend time alone and living in a virtual world. In such situations it is difficult for parents to monitor what children are watching.

* Parents parent in families where for much of the time they live in parallel rather than together so children have less opportunity to

learn and practise conversation skills, to explore ideas and values with their parents.

* Parents worry about crime and violence, drug use, education, what types of friends their children have and that their youngsters know about safe sex.

* Most parents have had little or no exposure to babies and young children until they have their own. They worry about doing the best for their children and how best to handle them. How to discipline children is a parenting issue that is quite high on their agenda. They also express concern about how they will manage to parent their children through the teenage years.

* Increased family disruption through separation, divorce and remarriage means that many parents go through emotional trauma while continuing to parent their children.

You may have other points that you would add to the list. However, from the fifteen that we have, we see that the contexts for parenting today are challenging, if not difficult. Most parents do a fine job in contexts like these but they do not necessarily feel that they do, so anything that can be done to affirm the good that they do and to help them to gain confidence as parents is important. As one grandmother wrote, 'I want to tell them what a good job they have done so far and to encourage them to carry on. I want to thank them for allowing me to be part of their lives.' And another wrote, 'I really admire the way they are bringing up the children.'

Other grandparents would like to offer some advice to busy parents:

'Try to appreciate your children. They grow up so quickly and we can be so busy that we do not appreciate the precious gift that we have.'

'We all make mistakes so do not be afraid to apologize to your children.'

'You (the particular parents being addressed) might find it helpful to be a little firmer occasionally.'

'Try to check what they watch on TV.'

'Always love them and be kind and honest, especially when they grow up.'

In my experience grandparents recognize that parents are doing their best. They remember what it is like to parent and see that today's world of parenting is probably more complex and fast-changing than the one in which they parented their children. Just as grandparents today are in new territory, so are parents.

There are resources and agencies available to help parents gain knowledge and understanding of their children and teenagers. There are others that will enable them to learn skills for parenting. Some of these are listed in the resources section of this book. Parents may sometimes value knowing about them. I heard a grandparent telling her daughter-in-law about gatherings that 'newish' parents were having in the church to explore parenting issues. 'I really would have valued such a group when I had young children,' she said.

Parents appreciate grandparents who are caring and co-operative, those they get along with relatively well, and who welcomed their son- or daughter-in-law into the family or, in the case of a cohabiting couple, the other partner. They are more likely to trust their children to their grandparents if they experienced them as loving and trusting parents. Parents flourish when they receive affirmation and praise but wither when destructive and unnecessary criticism comes their way. Most of them are vulnerable people who need encouragement. Much depends on the relationship between parents and grandparents. Kornhaber[2] suggests that the relationship works best when both can act in age-appropriate ways with the other.

'Granny and Grandad upset my Mum'

Of course, there are some parent/grandparent relationships that do not work so well and the reasons vary. It may be that a grandparent has an 'I have my life and they have theirs' attitude, or that the relationship in the past has been difficult, or that they have not handled differences of opinion in the past. If grudges are not dealt with, if there is bad personal chemistry between parents and grandparents, then the relationship may end in alienation unless the grandparents take the initiative to resolve the problem. I say grandparents because from both experience and research[2] it seems that it is usually the grandparents who take the initiative in remedying problems. Parents and grandchildren expect them to do so, perhaps because they think that age brings wisdom and/or authority.

Given the opportunity, most parents that I know value the involvement of grandparents in their children's lives. They and their children like it when grandparents can be actively involved in the lives of the children. They value the time that grandparents have and give, the outings and play, the chatting and stories, the indoor and outdoor games. When asked what they thought their children were learning from grandparents, a group of parents were quick to respond and grateful. Here is what they said:

'They are learning to be kind and accepting ... to share and be interested in others ... that people matter more than things ... to feel secure because they are appreciated ... to value their family ... to see old age positively ... to have social attitudes towards education, welfare and political action ... to argue and resolve conflict ... that God has an important place in the lives of their grandparents.'

From the responses given it is clear that the relationships between the parents and grandparents referred to are good, and that the grandparents are making a great contribution to the children's lives which the parents value. Another story can sometimes be told when grandparents hold different values from parents. A visitor to my home explained recently how difficult it was trying to educate your child to limit her intake of sweets when one set of grandparents have a 'sweet drawer' from which the children can help themselves. I suggested that it may be advisable to initiate a discussion with the grandparents to remedy the situation rather than to let the frustration increase.

Young children usually have two sets of grandparents and it is likely that they will learn different things from them because each household will have different rules and ways of doing things. One set of grandparents may be more active in supporting parents and grandchildren than another. 'We wish they would show more active interest,' wrote a couple about a set of grandparents who live closer to them than the more active ones who live three hundred miles away. It seems that many parents value their relationships with grandparents and have much for which to thank them.

Parents and grandparents

'Thank you for interest shown ... for sharing my joys and troubles ... for praying for us ... for being there ... for making time for holidays ... for devoting time to the children ... for being wise and understanding ... for supporting without being critical ... for loving and helping ... for being positive role-models ... for listening and including the children in 'adult conversation' ... for your ability to discuss relationships and feelings ... for being you and the quality of your personality.'

In our society there are some parents who are estranged from grandparents or who live a long way from them and they feel the need of support from an elder or honorary parent/grandparent. There are also older people in the community who have no grandchildren and who would value the opportunity of becoming involved in the lives of parents and children. In my local paper recently there was an advertisement with an accompanying photograph of a mum, probably in her thirties, and a child of about seven years. They were appealing for honorary grandparents. The child wanted grandparents to hand who would do all the things that grandparents do and the parent wanted an older generation in the family that would be mutually beneficial to her as a parent and to the honorary grandparents. Is there a seed of an idea here that might help to create community and enrich the lives of parents, children and older people who may not have the benefit of having family nearby?

Take Ten

Think about the parents of your grandchildren.

* ✽ What would you like to say to them to affirm them in what they are doing? Say it.

* ✽ What would you thank them for, given the opportunity? Write a note or tell them. They will experience it as affirmation.

* ✽ Identify differences in your past relationship that have been addressed. How have you remedied them? If they have not been addressed and are affecting relationships, plan to do something soon.

* ✽ Imagine that you are standing in the shoes of the parents of your grandchildren. What support or co-operation might they appreciate from you right now? What support and co-operation might you appreciate from them right now? Do what you can to make it happen.

A prayer for parents

Lord,

*Being a parent is a long and scary task
to undertake in the difficult context of these times.*

Please bless the parents of my grandchildren.

*Grant them health and wisdom and stamina
in their parenting,
and a good portion of fun, laughter and
satisfaction as they see their children grow.*

*Help them to avoid over-busy-ness so that they
can appreciate the precious gift of children.*

*Please enable me to respect them and co-operate
with them in the raising of their children, my
grandchildren.*

References

1 Pugh G, De'Ath E, Smith C, *Confident Parents, Confident Children* (National Children's Bureau 1994), p 40,

2 Kornhaber A, *Contemporary grandparenting* (Sage Publications 1996), pp 38, 86, 176.

Grandchildren — living in the world

Pat and Mike Johnston's grandchildren range in age from eighteen months to fourteen years. Sometimes Pat and Mike talk about 'the grandchildren' and at other times they talk about Emma or Amy or Jamie or Chloe or Matthew. Their grandchildren are growing up fast. They are at different stages of development, living in three unique families, each with their own personality. They are individuals living through the joys and trials of childhood and the early teenage years in a world that Pat and Mike feel is very different from the one in which they grew up. They would like to have a better understanding of that world.

Of all the subjects that I have been asked to address, by the grandparents consulted about this book, this is the one that has been mentioned most often. 'The world in which we grew up was so different to the one in which my grandchildren are growing up. I would like to understand it better.' A good place to begin is with our own childhood. What was childhood like when we were young?

Take Ten

Think about your own childhood and make notes on your reflections.

* What are your significant memories of your bedroom, your brothers and sisters, friends, schooldays, leisure time, i.e. games, activities, books, the media, your toys, clothes, pocket money, interests, holidays?

* Build up as comprehensive a picture as you can.

If we asked today's children to do a similar exercise I am sure that they would produce pictures that reveal some similarities in their experience of the world but there would be some major differences too. As we have seen in previous chapters, their experiences of family life and culture will differ. Family circumstances will affect how they live and the opportunities that they have. Life in the middle of a large housing estate on the edge of a big city is very different from life in the green leafy suburbs of the same city or, to put it another way, life on Front Street will be different from life on Back Street. While all children have intrinsic value, they live in a world of unequal opportunities. There are rich families and poor families, some that function well and others that do not do so well. All these factors will affect how children experience and view the world. Having said that, I believe that there are some general themes that it may be helpful to raise.

Parental expectations

The first theme is parental expectations. Some parents are anxious, sometimes determined, that their children do well at school — in every test from baseline assessment through to their final degree — and this can create pressure for children. Extra tuition may be obtained and children schooled for the next test. I remember a boy of eight whose parents were anxious that he did well in mathematics because they wanted him to inherit the family accountancy firm. He struggled with mathematics but enjoyed other subjects. The pressure was too great and he became clinically anxious, something from which he suffered for a long time. Then there was the mother who felt that her son must have a 'good start' in his education so she would make sure that he could read before starting school. Some children read earlier than others and the child felt the pressure. He learned to read but hardly looks at a book now unless he really needs to for a piece of work that he is doing. A lot of children live with too high expectations of them and that in turn creates pressure.

However, there are other children whose parents have low expectations of them, who do not expect their children to do well at school or to have ambitions. It may be that they had a poor experience of school themselves and do not value what is on offer. When their children do something well they may not recognize the achievement for what it is, or maybe there is no encouragement and affirmation of the children forthcoming from them. Then children may feel that parents do not care. When parents have too high or too low expectations of their children, the children suffer from the results of the pressure created and often from low self-esteem. Feelings of being loved conditionally can result, with children thinking that parental love depends on their achievements rather than on the fact that they are who they are and loved no matter what.

Taking the middle road with children may not be easy but it is important to try to do so. A warning for parents is: 'be aware of your expectations of children and the pressures you might place on them.' Children often feel that their grandparents are more easy-going and do not pressurize them in the same way. If that is the case then there is an important role for grandparents who are felt to love unconditionally.

Pressurized and hurried children

In addition, children live in a school world that has changed rapidly in recent years. They may well feel the effects of the pace of change and its impact on many teachers who themselves feel pressurized. At this point I am making no value judgement on the actual changes made — merely on the speed and process of the changes. If the adults with whom children spend time are pressurized, and perhaps insecure or tired, or feeling un-affirmed in their work, then it is easy to see that there may be spin-offs that are felt by the children. Children sense the emotional state of adults around them and pick up on feelings of pressure and insecurity. Of course, many teachers go the extra mile to ensure that children have a good time learning. Even so, the pressure felt by many children seems to be greater than that felt by most I know in my generation and I went to school in the days of weekly tests and class positions. Pressures for us came as we approached the eleven plus for which we were schooled and then labelled 'pass' or 'fail'. That pressure is now replicated every time children sit a national test and league tables are produced, i.e. at regular intervals through their childhood. I heard recently of a child who had been invited to join a mathematics group after school and his parents were pleased for him, feeling that the extra tuition was for his sake and would help him to become more numerate. However, the parents discovered that the primary motivation for the extra mathematics was to school him for his Standard Attainment Tests rather than to enable him to gain confidence with number and to increase his understanding of mathematics. The school was more concerned about its position in the published league tables than in the needs of the child. The parents felt cheated because they discerned that in this case the schooling for a test was not the same as enabling a child to learn mathematics.

There is a saying: 'If you don't know where you are going, you end up somewhere else.' I agree with it and am sure that there needs to be direction in children's education and that it is helpful to have a core curriculum that is common to all schools. Objectives are important but how these are understood, interpreted and implemented is equally important and that is where the rubber hits the road. It is also where children experience and feel the effects of the changes in education. Take, for instance, *Desirable Learning Outcomes for Children's Learning on Entering Compulsory Education*[1] i.e. the term in which they are five. This and other government documents emphasize the importance of play for children under five as a means of learning. The intentions are good but, in practice, workers in early childhood education often feel that there is less time for play in establishments that feel the pressure to get children literate and numerate. Emphasis is primarily on intellectual learning and development at a time when it is vital for children to be learning and growing emotionally, socially, spiritually and in every other way. So, children have less time to use their imaginations in play, to work through their questions and troubles, to practise being friends, etc. It seems that many children are pressurized and hurried to perform early in the areas of learning that are deemed to be important, while other areas of learning and development are receiving less time than they might deserve. In my view one of these areas is talking or conversation skills. In most continental countries children do not begin full-time schooling until they are six or seven years of age and they learn to read in about three months, probably because they have had an excellent nursery experience and are ready. In England and Wales many Pre-school Learning Alliance groups are closing. They have always emphasized play. Schools are taking children in earlier (as early as three-and-a-half) and placing them in classes where there are fewer adults with the children than in pre-school groups. In addition, in many of these situations primary, rather than nursery, ways of doing things are practised. When this happens young children are not only being pressurized, they are being hurried through their childhood — often from the best of motives.

It is not only the under-fives who are hurried. As one parent indicated: 'The children have something on every evening except one — swimming, dancing, music, Brownies. They lead busy lives with homework too.' Sometimes children can be so stimulated that they feel pressurized or cannot relax and at others they can be so under-stimulated that they do not learn. Again keeping the balance is important and so is encouraging them to do some things for the sheer enjoyment of doing them.

Children often share their lives with parents who are in a hurry too. Reports in recent newspapers indicate that stress is a problem for parents trying to juggle work with home-making and parenting. Again this has implications for relationships, including those with children who can easily become the recipients of sharp words from tired and stressed parents. Sometimes there is little real interaction or communication between parents and their children, especially with fathers — an estimated 30-60 seconds a day! Pressurized, hurried, stressed — is it any wonder that a recent report from the Mental Health Association said that one in five children today suffer from a stress-related illness?

Less freedom

Caring parents, and that is most parents, want to protect their children from danger and to ensure that they are safe. Juggling the family 'taxi service' and working with a complicated timetable of taking children to and from their activities is a feature of family life that can add to the time pressures. However, this is not an issue in families where money is tight and the extra activities are not an option. When you were young, perhaps you had the freedom to walk to school with your friends, to play in the park or the street, to go for walks in the woods or whatever. Today's children have less freedom for safety reasons. Parents fear for their safety, and rightly so, though the irony is that children are at greater risk of abuse from family members than from those outside the family. Parents are concerned that their children will play with the 'wrong people', get into drugs, or be unsafe crossing roads, or be the victims of violence and so some children are well into the secondary school years before they are allowed to find their own way to school. It is true that there are some welcome initiatives to create safe spaces for children but, until they are in place, children have little opportunity for unsupervised free play.

Take Ten

**394 parents were asked, 'Thinking about your children,
please tell me which, if any, of the following particularly worry you as a parent?'
The top ten answers were:**

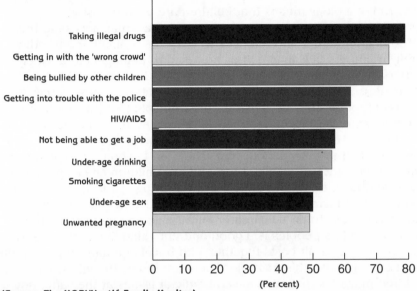

(Source: The MORI/Nestlé Family Monitor)

Sometimes fear can be alleviated when there is relevant information to hand. Take a few minutes to make phone calls or write brief letters to obtain information that might help you or the parents of your grandchildren, e.g. The National Drugs Helpline (0800 77 66 00) has a helpful booklet: *A Parents' Guide to Drugs and Solvents.*

While many children may have less freedom of movement than in previous generations, they are able to find their way across the television channels and to surf the 'net' so that they have access to information and knowledge at the push of a button. They are confident with hard- and software, unlike many grandparents who were brought up without computers and the like. On the whole they are unafraid of the new technology and increasingly have their own televisions and computers in their bedrooms. The current generation of children usually have their own bedrooms kitted out not only with IT equipment but with every kind of toy imaginable. Rather than the one or two soft

87

toys, often home-made, that their grandparents had, they have shelves full as well as all kinds of plastic and brightly coloured toys that have been well marketed to them, their parents and other relatives. Many children probably have more toys than they can possibly benefit from — they live in an increasingly materialistic society.

Modern technology means that children are used to instant communication. For instance, my nieces have e-mail access to their paternal grandfather and relatives who live in Trinidad and to other family members in Canada. They are used to belonging to a widely dispersed, multi-cultural family with roots in Chinese, Trinidadian, Portuguese, and English (north and south) cultures. Perhaps they are an exception but they do illustrate the principle that the world has become a smaller place, a global village, as fascinating as it ever was for children. They are aware of some of the great issues that face the world. In their primary school years they can become real campaigners with a great sense of justice. I have known children challenge parents and grandparents to more ethical ways of living — for the sake of the planet — and increasing numbers seem to become vegetarians once they can choose to do so. Greater knowledge and understanding of the world and its peoples is a good and enriching thing. Easier and relatively cheaper air costs together with travel and nature programmes on television make this possible. There are times, though, when children may be exposed to several difficult issues at the same time, such as famine, wars, loss of the rain forests and devastation by hurricanes. Then many worry and it can add to any sense of insecurity they may already have. Obviously, if there are opportunities to talk about their concerns, they can be helped to feel that there is hope for the world and to be involved in sensitive social action that will help them as activists (which most are) to feel that they are doing something. Programmes like the BBC's *Blue Peter* are good at helping them to do this.

Children's ease with both the computer and the Internet opens up a whole new world to them. They can 'meet' new friends through it, relate through the e-mail and develop virtual relationships. The value of these things has to be monitored. It is early days but perhaps the information technology revolution has affected or is affecting children's lives more than any other area of change. With every change come some gains and some losses. In some changes the gains outweigh the losses, and sometimes it is the other way round. In my view there are many benefits for children in using information technology but, like everything else, it has to be used wisely and selectively. Children can become addicted to computer games and there are fears that parents are unable to monitor which web sites children access, or indeed which programmes they watch on television, because they watch them in the privacy of their own rooms. In the early years it may be helpful to have a policy of selective viewing with children and to talk about what is watched together. Making more television viewing a shared and discussed activity will help to train children to select what they watch, partly because that is a norm in their household and partly because they learn to discern what certain types of programmes are doing to them. More shared activity may also help to counteract the 'living in parallel syndrome' that occurs when everyone has their own room with their own TV, computer, work station, etc. and where little time is spent together nurturing relationships and learning and practising interpersonal skills.

Between many television programmes come the advertisements, and in recent years children and young people have increasingly become targets of the marketing moguls. Through other forms of advertising, parents are persuaded to buy expensive designer clothes for growing children. Children pressurize their parents for the latest designer trainers at £80–£100 a go. To have street credibility is important to children even in primary schools and they often know which designer label they require. A mother I know discovered some top brand trainers for sale at a much reduced price in a local shoe shop. (They were seconds but the flaws hardly showed.) She felt that she could afford a pair for her daughter's Christmas present. The gift was warmly received but a few days later her daughter was attacked. Some peers wanted her trainers because they had the 'right' label on them.

Violence is one of the things that parents worry about most. A cub/scout leader told me recently that his pack no longer plays the games it did eight or ten years ago. He was talking about wide games like Shipwreck. The reason he gave was that the boys had become too physically violent. When one player was caught by an opposing team it was now 'normal' for the boys to use fists and feet as a matter of course. This is disturbing news. Sometimes children do not differentiate between fantasy and fact, and sometimes the two are muddled in the television, films, etc. that they see. It is a violent world that is portrayed to them and certainly a fiercely competitive one. A competitive spirit is encouraged by many. The world admires winners and not losers. Perhaps more help needs to be given to encourage co-operation between children. There are many co-operative games that can be played but it will take an attitude change and real effort on the part of adults to change the climate. Children desperately need good role-models, especially boys who may spend little time with adult men.

An exercise that you might like to undertake would be to adjust some of the games that you play with grandchildren so that they become co-operative rather than competitive. It might also help if adults consciously praise children for helpful and co-operative activity so that they come to realize that they receive notice and affirmation for that. It is the experience of some children that bad behaviour brings attention when otherwise there would be none — for them a reprimand can be better than no attention at all.

A friend told me recently that his son had decided that the best way to survive school was to appear not to work. If he worked and appeared to co-operate with teachers then he would be the subject of ridicule, of teasing or bullying. Bullying is a problem in many schools and if you want to read about its effects I suggest that you read Charlie Irvine's account of bullying in *Family and All That Stuff*[2]. There must be a number of reasons why some children are bullied and some are bullies. It is my belief that both bullied and bully have one thing in common and that is low self-esteem. (It may be that some of the bullied acquire low self-esteem as a result of the bullying.) However, there are many other children who also suffer from low self-esteem — those who have undergone or who are undergoing family trauma, those who feel pressurized or hurried, those who are rarely affirmed, and so the list goes on. If I had to identify a major problem for today's children it would be low self-esteem and it may be that grandparents can help to remedy the situation for some children by enhancing their images of themselves and by encouraging parents to do the same. How soon do we hear them saying, 'I can't do it,' or 'I'm no good at it'? So often they do not feel valued and that is terrible, a denial of the Good News as I understand it. In section three of this book we pick up some ways that we can help children to feel better about themselves.

A question that is asked at intervals through life is: 'Who am I?' and children are no exception. They spend a lot of time trying to work out an answer to the question because they need a sense of identity. That is one reason why the family story is so important. It helps them to know their 'story so far' and to sense that as they live their lives so they add to their story. Children today live in a more multi-cultural and multi-faith society than previous generations. This makes it doubly important that they know their story — but also that they know the stories of other people and learn to respect them and how they find their identity. If racism and other prejudices are to be addressed in society then the nurturing of children's friendships is to be encouraged — they share classrooms and play spaces. It is when people meet and share their lives that attitudes and values change and when prejudice and stereotypical views are shattered. Children from different ethnic and social backgrounds share their classrooms and play spaces and, sometimes, homes. Modern children are in places where friendship, understanding and mutual respect can be encouraged and where fears of difference might be addressed.

While the world in which children are growing up is different from the one which their parents or grandparents experienced, childhood for children today is the only world that they have known. It is the world as they know it — in which they grow, explore, develop friendships, learn and mature. They journey through their stages of childhood reaching the natural milestones (like walking) that all generations have reached before them and they dance to different music. In fact they dance to a whole range of different styles of music and develop their own language. As a fourteen-year-old said, 'My brothers like heavy metal but I'm into Indie myself.' An illustration of the different or the developing language of children and young people came to me when a worried grandparent told me about a child who had told him, 'Jesus is wicked.' In fact the child was using a word that has been given new meaning, almost the opposite of its original meaning, and was paying Jesus a great compliment.

Take Ten

* Make a cup of tea or coffee. Turn on the radio to a channel that your grandchildren listen to. Put your feet up and listen. Alternatively watch *Top of the Pops*. Is there anything that surprises you about what you hear and see?

* Ask a grandchild if you can borrow a favourite CD or cassette. Play it and read the words of the songs. Recall some of the songs that you sang in your teens. What are the values and concerns expressed in the modern songs? Are they similar to or different from the ones that were conveyed through your music and songs?

Different does not mean worse. It is worth remembering that many people who are grandparents now lived through some difficult years in their childhood with wars or Cold Wars, threats of atom bombs, ration books and absent fathers who were away with the armed forces.

Today's children live in their context and it is helpful for grandparents to understand it so that they can offer appropriate and sometimes mutual support. However they do not need to understand every detail of a youngster's world because, as one who wanted some space put it: 'I love my grandparents. I don't need them to like my music, or understand everything or even know or use some of the words I do.' But, as many have expressed, they do appreciate grandparents who are 'there for them', giving time, offering listening ears and wise words, and helping them to feel accepted and secure because grandparents have been in their world as long as they have known it. As one child wrote: 'They are older than Mum and Dad and not so busy ... If I could give them any present in the world I would build a house with a granny annexe so that when they get really old we can look after them.'

Prayer

Lord,

We all know that the journey of life is sometimes easy and sometimes hard.

As one who shares part of the journey of my grandchildren, help me to be there for them in ways that they find supportive.

Bless them as they travel. Keep them safe.

Give them enough time to explore, to play, to stop and stare, to laugh and relax.

Please enable adults (parents, grandparents, teachers, decision-makers) to remember that children need to travel at their own pace and to learn to adjust their steps accordingly.

References

1 *Nursery Education: Desirable outcomes for children's learning on entering compulsory education* (DFEE, Crown Copyright, Revised and reprinted 1998)

2 King J (ed), *Family and all that stuff* (NCEC 1998)

Section 3:
What can a grandparent do?

Grandparenting from a distance

Distance from grandchildren is a major concern for increasing numbers of grandparents. For about one quarter of them, seeing grandchildren involves a two-hour journey, for others it includes an air flight as more people are scattered around the global village. Often they ask: 'Is it possible to grandparent effectively from a distance?' Obviously they cannot be on hand in a physical sense like grandparents who are 'local' but with modern communication and ease of travel, it is easier than it used to be to keep in contact.

It is good to talk and most of us have at our disposal a telephone, possibly a fax machine and increasingly the electronic mail. As one grandparent said, 'I talk to my granddaughter in America almost daily. We use e-mail now but she used to like the fax machine. I really enjoyed receiving her drawings and illustrated messages.' Electronic mail means that communication is almost instant and closes the gap that miles between people create. Another friend explained that he was able to keep in regular touch with grandchildren living in East Africa. 'We have some wonderful conversations via e-mail and I am learning a lot about life in East Africa.'

However, the most popular way of keeping in touch with grandchildren and sustaining relationships is by telephone. There is an art to conversing on the telephone. It requires good communication skills in the absence of some of the normal clues/cues that we receive when talking face to face. Children have to learn to use the telephone but they usually take to it like a duck to water because they cannot remember life without it. Adults sometimes find conversing with younger grandchildren a strain. This is

95

because children have insufficient verbal language to express themselves but they enjoy hearing your voice saying 'hello' and addressing them by name or even saying a goodnight prayer with them. As they grow they usually like to hear your news and to tell you what they have been doing. In my experience children really value these communications.

The telephone is part of everyday life but to hear the thump of a letter or parcel landing on the doormat — well, that is marvellous. I still have a postcard sent to me by one of my elders when I was eight years old. He sent it from Malaya during the monsoon season and described his experience of being in torrential rain. At the time it was a source of wonder to me that this card had come half way round the world and it fuelled in me a life-long interest in geography. Similarly children today are thrilled to receive communications through the post that are specifically addressed to them. Most of us send birthday cards and Christmas cards but postcards and short letters using clear handwriting can add some magic to your relationship and enhance your significance in children's lives because by sending them you are saying implicitly, 'I am thinking of you and you matter to me.' And it works the other way too.

To receive a first scribble, a hand- or footprint, or a drawing through the post usually brings a smile of joy to the receiver and no doubt the sender has enjoyed sealing the envelope, sticking on the stamp and taking it to the post-box. Somehow the contents of an envelope or a telephone conversation help people to feel closer.

When my nephews and nieces were younger they wondered what would be the best Christmas present to send to their grandparents who lived in Trinidad. They decided to write and illustrate a 'Family Annual' in which they would describe some of the high- and lowlights of their year in England. They described their first Scripture Union camp, their activities in the cubs, going in the ambulance to 'have stitches' after falling off a bike. Poems and imaginative stories were included and the baby made her own contribution — some pages of scribble. They interviewed their Mum and Dad and wrote about their other relatives. The annual was a great success, so much so that it was reproduced for great-aunts and -uncles, friends and relatives even though it was written with grandparents in mind. Some twenty years later that booklet is still in existence. It meant a lot both to those living thousands of miles away and to those living a couple of hundred miles down the motorway.

Since then I have often thought how affirming it would be for grandchildren, especially those living at a distance, to receive such gifts from their grandparents. They would give children permanent records, part of their family story, and convey something of the personalities, values and interests of their grandparents. Through them children would get to know their grandparents better. They would have something tangible to add to their experiences of their grandparents and to take with them through life's journey.

Take Ten

* Imagine that you are going to make a booklet or an annual for your grandchildren about yourself and your life in the last year. What would be the highlights that you would include? What would be the lowlights? Which photographs, cards, theatre/cinema/football programmes, illustrations etc. might you include? Have you any funny stories or jokes to include? What would you want to share about yourself? What would you call the booklet and what design would you give to the cover?

* Note down your thoughts. Block out some time in your diary to make the booklet. Do it — it could be fun!

While grandparents, living at a distance, may have to be creative in sustaining relationships with grandchildren using every means available to them, there is no doubt that they can be extremely significant and influential people. There are enough young adults around to testify to this. Many speak not only of telephone contact and letters but of the special visits they made at regular intervals to stay with grandparents. They tell of quality time, special places and customs. Sometimes it is as if the ordinary becomes extraordinary to the children. 'I remember Nan's big teapot. We used to drink tea and sit and talk for ages.' 'I remember gardening with Grandad. He showed me how to make compost.' And sometimes the memories are of being able to do things with grandparents that normally were not allowed!

'I remember going in the mud by the Severn estuary with Grandad and my brothers. We were covered in mud by the time we had finished, throwing soft mud balls like snowballs. Grandad said it didn't matter if we were muddy. The mud would

*wash off at home — not in the river because that was too
dangerous.'*

For those living at a distance from grandchildren there is the
opportunity of spending regular time with most grandchildren in
school holidays and the like. Sometimes these visits have to fit
around the grandparents' paid work but their value should not be
underestimated. Even those with grandchildren living nearby can offer
the occasional sleepover that gives added value to the children's
visits. Children look forward to such experiences and feel valued
because grandparents have time and do not appear to hurry them as
others do. The experiences are often of mutual acceptance, of fun, of
unconditional love.

Daniel, who is five, wrote of his grandparents:

*'They live a long, long, long way away (three hundred miles). We
sometimes go on the train. Grandad grows rhubarb and
raspberries. Granny cooks dinner and PUDDING.'*

He drew a picture of two tiny figures standing by an enormous railway
track that spoke eloquently of the physical distance between him and
his grandparents. The means of travel and of meeting featured highly
and this is perhaps indicative of the warmth and depth of their love
for each other. Phone, fax, post and the railway help them to sustain
their relationships.

Grandad and Granny waiting at the station to come and see me.
They live a long way away.

Daniel's experiences are similar to those of some young adults I know. Throughout their childhood their grandparents' home became a special place with lots of associations and good memories. When their grandparents were older and needing more support they moved to live near their children and grandchildren. The gain of having grandparents nearby was also marked by the loss of that special, almost holy place, and the realization that Nana and Grandad who were the hub of the extended family would not always be around. The move marked a time of new beginnings for everyone and adjustments were made in relationships as adult grandchildren and adult grandparents lived in closer proximity, enjoying regular discussions and watching sport together on television. They had a bond and genuine interest in each other that had been nurtured across the miles for over twenty years and enriched through regular holidays together.

When children have such positive experiences of interested and loving grandparents, even from a distance, they fill out the meaning of the name Granny or Grandad. Their own identities and attitudes are developed in relation to themselves and the older people in their lives. Sadly when grandchildren perceive that grandparents do not genuinely enjoy their company even from a distance then their images of them remain flat or hollow. As one person told me, 'We did not really relate. My only memory of my grandmother is that she ate "Energen Rolls".' Can you remember those bland bread substitutes, popular as slimming aids in the 1960s?

So if you are in a position of having grandchildren who live some distance away, consider what you are doing, and could do further, to sustain your relationships with them and, for that matter, with their parent(s). Be assured that you can be significant in their lives as they can in yours, and it is important that you are, because you are their living ancestor.

I was cheered when visiting the home of a prospective grandmother. Her grandchild would be living three hours' drive away. 'Mum's been in the attic,' I was told. I found her in the kitchen showing her son and daughter-in-law some of her attic-finds — a carry-cot, cot sheets and other baby paraphernalia. Together they were ensuring that there would be enough of the basic essentials at Grandma's house to make weekend visits easy. Mum, son and daughter-in-law were working together on their shifts into the next generation and preparing for their new roles which would be undertaken across the miles via the telephone but with regular, quality visits to each other's homes. All three were looking forward to having a new person in the family though they recognized that life would never be the same once the child arrived. A new baby offers grandparents the opportunity of a new relationship that can be nurtured creatively even when they live miles apart.

A prayer for grandparents and grandchildren separated by distance

Lord,
The miles stretch between them, separating them
but if we look closely we see the signs...

Telephone wires
The Royal Mail van
'Phones, faxes and e-mail
Aeroplanes.

They are the lifelines that keep them together
like the umbilical cord that links baby to mother.

Thank you for the wonders
of modern communication.
Please help grandparents and grandchildren
to be creative in using the tools
that are available to them.
May they come to know one another well
and may they enrich each other's lives
as they grow through their experiences
of being linked across the miles.

Playing with grandchildren

A my and Emma Foster joined forces with their parents in buying a present to mark their grandparents' Ruby Wedding. Their parents asked them to consider what would make a good present for their grandparents. For weeks they talked about what they might buy. They wanted it to be something that Pat and Mike Johnston would really enjoy and something that would help them to express their love to their grandparents. After several evenings browsing through catalogues they decided that a compendium of games would be appropriate. Why? As they planned they found themselves reminiscing about their grandparents, what they liked doing with them, and what they appreciated about them. They remembered the presents that had come from England — the toys, games and books — and they remembered the times they had spent with their grandparents in Africa and England. Much of that time, as far as they could remember, was spent playing. They still enjoyed playing with them on the computer, and with word games and puzzles, but some of their board games were now worn out or had pieces missing. Yes, they would buy their grandparents some games so that they could play — even play with them, their parents and the younger grandchildren when they visited. Their parents agreed with their suggestion and also bought a little table, just the right height for playing games when sitting in a comfortable chair.

The fond memory of grandparents as playful people, as people who will put their own agenda to one side and stop to play with you, is typical of those people who have had a warm, positive experience of grandparents. According to the responses I have received, playing with grandchildren is one of the most significant things that grandparents can do, whether it is kicking a ball around with a grandchild or entering into some form of imaginative play. Play is vitally important and used to be called 'the work of children.' It can promote their growth and development in every way — physical, intellectual, linguistic, emotional, social and spiritual growth — and yet play is often devalued in modern society where everyone is in a hurry and children's activities are designed to meet goals. Having a home where children can play alone, together and with you, and being prepared to spend time playing when visiting them, is one of the best gifts that grandparents can give to their grandchildren. By doing so they affirm them and show their real interest in them, they show that they like being with their grandchildren, they laugh, they explore imaginative worlds, they encounter the world and discover how things work. As Tina Bruce, author of several books on early childhood education, said on a recent radio programme, 'Grandparents are wonderfully relaxed teachers.' They enable children to learn and develop by playing.

'My Nan laughs until tears run down her face'

How and with what children play will vary as they grow. With a baby grandparents might unconsciously play with facial expressions and tone of voice as they 'chat' or sing. Stimulating objects to watch, to feel and taste encourage grandchildren to explore the world around them and to have a variety of tactile and visual experiences. As they reach the crawling, walking and toddling stages there may be physical challenges provided, e.g. climbing stairs. Visits to the park will encourage the use of big muscles that need exercise through play and the play is usually so much more fun if the adult joins in. Activities like threading cotton reels will exercise small muscles and encourage hand and eye co-ordination. I favour the use of ordinary, household objects where possible. We all know of children who receive wonderful presents intended for a specific purpose but who gain more satisfaction from the wrapping paper and packaging.

Younger children are natural explorers who are curious to find out how the world works, so safe exploration is important. One grandmother I know had a cupboard in her kitchen that was available for exploring. While the other base units had childproof locks this one did not. Her grandchildren (two boys) soon learned the boundaries — one cupboard was for them. The cupboard contained real household equipment — sets of saucepans that would fit inside one another if they were placed in the right order, lids that fitted specific saucepans, jugs, colanders, sieves and tools of similar shapes but different sizes. All were safe, unbreakable and with smooth edges. The boys spent hours exploring the equipment, sometimes alone, sometimes together and sometimes with their grandmother. She would intervene to help them along with the sorting and fitting of lids. Often they would play alongside her while she prepared vegetables and then they would help her to wash the vegetables in the colander and to decide which saucepan to use when cooking them. Through such simple activities they were playing with mathematical ideas, learning to co-operate with their grandmother and each other (and sometimes to resolve their squabbles) and to be involved in making some reasonable decisions. They also learned to replace the items in the cupboard at first with their grandmother and later by themselves, thus learning to take responsibility for their playthings — at least for some of the time!

Sometimes a bowl of water would be offered or requested and some of the contents of the cupboard would be used in water play. Then the children would concentrate as they poured water from jugs into sieves and filled saucepans before emptying them to start the process over again. When the children were a little older the play developed and they became 'workmen' and the sieves etc. started to become other objects for the purpose of the play. When this happens we say that children are using symbols.

A favourite play provision is the dressing-up box that might also contain a few props. Children love to dress up and to role-play. This type of play helps them to replay what they know of people, to step into other people's shoes and to work things out about them. Many an adult has observed their own character being 'played out' by their children in socio-dramatic play. Playing mummies and daddies is a favourite activity that enables children to explore their understanding of the world of home. Sometimes grandparents (or other adults) can be engaged in the play too, appreciating the cups of tea and the pretend meals served, and stimulating conversation while in role. When the role-play moves to the 'hospital', or the 'shops' the grandparent might become a 'patient' or a 'shopper'. By encouraging such play grandparents influence children's creativity, their language and intellectual growth, their social skills and sometimes their moral development as they learn to take turns, or to be fair or kind or caring in their play. There can sometimes be a therapeutic element to the play too.

I remember 'going fishing' with two boys aged four and five. The orange lounge carpet was the sea and the sofa was an ocean-going vessel. Cardboard boxes became the lifeboats and we had a 'drill' about what to do in an emergency. The 'drill' idea came from me but the other ideas came from the children and I co-operated. On board were some fishing lines (sticks and wool). The children wore baseball hats and I had a pirate-type scarf. Off we went on our adventure, through storms with all the accompanying sound effects and wave movements, to far-off places. We were a long way from home and we had forgotten to bring food. What could we do? We discussed our problem. The boys lowered the lifeboats and took the fishing lines, leaving me in charge of the big vessel. They 'rowed' over the orange sea and sat bobbing up and down while they cast their fishing lines. It was not long before they were hauling in the 'fish'. They returned to the big vessel and we had a 'fish meal' before sailing safely home through calmer seas.

We were all tired when we returned to port. This kind of fantasy play is hard work but it is important for a number of reasons. Through it children (and the adults involved) are using their imaginations, facing difficult, even dangerous situations in the security of a home and in a safe way. The boys braved the elements, they solved a problem and they 'left home' going further away than they had ever been, before returning home safely. In reality, one of the most important developmental tasks that we all have is to learn to leave home. We leave at different times in a variety of ways — the toddler toddles away and returns to a parent, the child goes for a sleepover with a friend and returns home, the teenager goes off to college or the young adult gets married. In their play these boys had a practice run at what can be a hard task emotionally. They left home (the security of the port) but returned safely having faced several challenges on the way. All was well.

Never undervalue play like this. It is powerful stuff that will happen if the props are there and the adults go along with it, sometimes offering a suggestion that will help the play to develop. Rich experiences of stories and books, of videos and activities, will extend the children's world and spark ideas in children that they develop. A positive, encouraging attitude towards this type of play is necessary. Children learn at a surprisingly early age what the significant adults in their lives really value and will adjust their behaviour accordingly. Therefore, if imaginative and fantasy play is not encouraged, children will opt for a quiet life and are likely to become bored or compliant. However, if they are encouraged to have ideas and to exercise their imaginations in play, they are likely to be creative and articulate, to be able to imagine the effects of their own and other people's actions, to feel how others feel, to work through some emotional challenges and to grow up with a sense of wonder as they play with ideas and observe the world around them.

In a world of hurried children I see a great contribution that grandparents can offer and that is to make time to play and/or to encourage play in informal, gentle ways. Grandparents need no curriculum, the play is the thing — it is the children's natural way and they will do it if they are stimulated to do so by people who value the play way and encourage it. To provide opportunities for rich experiences of play is an important, if not vital, role if children are to grow healthily in body, mind and spirit.

Take Ten

Think of your home environment. What is there to stimulate young children (under-eights) to play — objects, toys, spaces, equipment?

∗ Think of your wardrobes, attic, cupboards and drawers. What could you find in them to create or add to a stimulating dressing-up box? Are there friends who may donate items to extend the dressing-up opportunities, e.g. some African beads, an Indian sari, an Australian 'cork hat', an American baseball cap?

∗ Which areas of your home might you designate for young explorers like the boys with the saucepans?

∗ What might you provide from around your home to stimulate some impromptu socio-dramatic play about home and family?

Playing with grandchildren

As children grow they will move through stages in their play. This is linked in some ways to their social development, i.e. when they have learned to be friends and to play together. Until a certain amount of learning has occurred, children will play alone or alongside others, and will often engage in a lot of 'trial and error' play, e.g. putting shapes into a Shapes Ball. As children learn skills in other areas so they will learn to play more sophisticated board games, word games and eventually team games — for that they need to be emotionally mature enough to take their place in a team, which takes a lot of practice and learning. A grandparent who plays ball regularly with young grandchildren is hardly aware of the significance of what is being done. Abstract ideas like 'up and down', 'fast and slow', 'high and low' are being played with in concrete ways but also foundational learning is occurring about what it means to play together and eventually be a team player. It is probable that attitudes to 'winning' and 'losing' are being communicated and values about co-operation and competitiveness are being imbibed. And all this influence comes from simple but repeated games with a ball played by grandparents (or other significant adults) and their grandchildren! So we see the power of play and its potential influence on children's learning and development. By encouraging play, grandparents can promote their grandchildren's growth.

As grandchildren mature so do grandparents and it may be that grandparents come to a point when they can no longer be so actively involved in boisterous play. That is OK. Children accept that the knees are too stiff for Granny or Grandad to sit cross-legged on the floor any more. However, it is still possible for grandparents to encourage children and to be actively interested, or to take a special role that their special needs require, e.g. to spin the wheel for a game of Twister while the youngsters make the complicated physical moves. It is also possible to engage in the quieter, less energetic games that extend thinking, use of language, visual and spatial awareness, reasoning, problem-solving. Here I am thinking of puzzles, jigsaws, mapping games, counting games, storytelling games and the like. Many of these games can be enjoyed in different forms throughout life and they help to keep us mentally alert whatever our age. So keep playing.

Pat and Mike Johnston were thrilled with the games that they were given. They brought hours of fun and enjoyment, not only for them but for their grandchildren too. And that meant that they could expect some good times together in the future. They had always kept a box of special toys and games to use with the grandchildren when they visited as well as the dressing-up box and a special tent that the younger children used as a kind of den. In it the children created all sorts of imaginative play situations. Occasionally they invited their grandparents into it for a special 'picnic meal' and in a funny way they felt honoured when this happened. They had come to appreciate the sounds of children playing and the way that involvement in the play enabled them to see the world afresh through children's eyes and sometimes to observe how the children were feeling or thinking. Being grandparents with children who visited their home quite regularly meant that Pat and Mike could put energy into playing with their grandchildren knowing that at the end of the day the house would be back to normal and they had time to rest. Those grandparents whose grandchildren are unable to visit might still encourage play through their interest when talking to grandchildren on the telephone and through the toys and games that they buy as gifts.

Take Ten

Think about the following. Many toys are expensive and are designed to have only one kind of use. Some have a good, specific and limited purpose like encouraging hand and eye co-ordination but many do not. Neither do they stimulate the use of the imagination, so many households end up with a whole plastic play kitchen which for much of the time just takes up space because children do not want to play with it all the time. Sometimes it can be much more creative to make equipment or to use household objects to symbolize other things rather like the boys who used cardboard boxes as lifeboats. So think of as many items as possible that a cardboard box could be used to represent in play situations.

Now do the same exercise with the following items: a scarf, a stick, a plastic mug.

Prayer

Lord, it is wonderfully refreshing to hear the laughter of children as they play.

It is delightful to see them 'lost' in the small world of an imaginary game or to join them on an imaginary adventure or to see them imitating those they love or to observe them exploring dangerous and evil things through the safety of play or to recognize that they are rehearsing for their future and discovering how the world works.

Lord, children work so hard in their playing.

Thank you for what we adults can learn from them as they play in our midst —

the new insights, the refreshing questions, the honesty, the sense of awe and wonder.

Help us to retain our playfulness and to remain childlike so that we can see with wonder and awe the world that you have made, and recognize afresh how it works in the light of your Good News.

Everyday activities with grandchildren

Matthew Johnston liked the days when he went to Granny and Grandad's house. It felt warm, cosy and safe and there was a box of toys and a dressing-up box, as well as the garden to play in. He had his own coat peg that Grandad had put up for him — at a height that he could reach — and he knew that there would be plenty to do. It all felt like play to him, even when he helped with household chores or gardening or taking the dog for a walk. Life was fun, full of interest with new things to do and to discover and his grandparents were there encouraging, joining in, showing him things, appreciating him and just loving him. Many of these things he could not have put into words at the age of four. It just felt good being with them.

Pat and Mike Johnston enjoyed the days when Matthew came to their home while his mother worked. Like many grandparents they were the chief providers of childcare for their grandson while his Mum, Charlie, worked and studied. It was their way of supporting their daughter and her son whom they loved very much, but it was not something that they had dreamed of doing as they planned for their retirement. In the circumstances it was what they wanted to do and, as Mike often said in the evenings when they reflected on their day, 'Young Matthew is certainly keeping us young.' They appreciated having him with them but were glad to 'put their feet up' when he had returned home to his mother. Matthew helped them to see the world with fresh eyes. He was at that stage when questions flowed and when 'Because I said so' was an inadequate answer. Sometimes he challenged their thinking and sometimes he slowed them down so that they looked at and appreciated more of the world around them. They had found that they needed a gentle routine with Matthew. The coat peg had been a success. Their time with him always began with a drink and a chat. They would talk about what they had been doing and make plans for the day so that they would know what the fixed points were. For instance, on the day when library books were to be changed they would all go to the library early, do some shopping and have a mid-morning drink at the supermarket café before returning home. Then there were choices. Matthew might help to prepare lunch, play alone with some toys, do some drawings, 'read' his books with a grandparent or help with the gardening. It seemed that the day flowed with some fixed points in it. They always sat at the table for lunch at roughly the same time, kept the toys etc. in the same place, had routines for hand washing and rules about covering surfaces before painting or drawing. Rules, however, were kept to a minimum. Sometimes one or both grandparents would join Matthew in his play and sometimes he would join them in 'helping activities' like washing the car. Often these activities were made more fun by Matthew's presence but his grandparents had learned to allow more time than they would have required if doing the tasks alone.

Activities that Matthew and his grandparents enjoyed included:

Baking and cooking

Matthew had his own apron for when he helped to prepare food. Often his Granny would show him what to do and he would copy her. He loved to scrub potatoes when preparing them for baking, or to watch while vegetables were being prepared and then wash them. He liked making sandwiches — spreading the butter and choosing the fillings. He especially enjoyed weighing ingredients, rolling out pastry and putting jam into tarts or helping to make the icing to decorate cakes.

Matthew's older cousins also liked baking, and progressed to using more advanced equipment and tools. The teenagers are now able to plan and cook meals and sometimes prepare the meal when their grandparents visit their home.

Through these activities, Matthew and his cousins before him learned by observing adults, and by having a go. They were also introduced to new words (a lot of talking takes place during these activities) and experienced early chemistry lessons as they mixed ingredients for a cake or prepared icing to decorate it. Following a recipe helped them to learn how to plan and organize — essential skills for almost any job from homemaking to computer programming to high-powered researching.

Creative activities

Often Matthew would engage in a number of creative activities during a day. Paint, crayon, scissors (the right size for him), glue and a variety of papers (brown wrapping paper, used computer paper, gift wrap, tissue) were always to hand. So were boxes of junk for modelling, and scraps of wool and fabric left over from Granny's sewing and knitting projects. With these Matthew created models and pictures for his Mum and for display on Granny's fridge. He played with colours, patterns and design. Sometimes he drew and painted pictures to show what he had seen or what he had been doing. At other times it was the process of doing something that fascinated him, like cutting and sticking and using glitter or shiny paper. On days when he was feeling upset or unwell he found playdough (a home-made variety made from flour, salt, water and colouring) comforting and he could take out his feelings on it if he wanted to without hurting anyone. He was not bothered so much about the end result as the process of making or doing. Pat and Mike had learned the hard way with their grandchildren not to assume that they knew what a picture showed. Instead they gave Matthew opportunities to talk about what he had done. Occasionally one of them would introduce a new piece of equipment such as corrugated paper or coloured glitter glue or a new idea such as potato printing, or bubble painting, or wheel painting, i.e. using the wheels of small toys. There was so much for him to do in this area. He loved it and especially enjoyed those times when one or both of his grandparents worked alongside him, like on the day when they all made birthday cards for his Mum.

Friends

Sometimes friends of Matthew's grandparents came to the house for a coffee. He loved to hear them chatting and laughing. He observed how his grandparents behaved with friends from the church, those who came to visit and those they met in the library or the shop. His grandparents knew a lot of people. They were friendly. Sometimes visitors to the house would bring a child who would play with Matthew, at other times his cousin Chloe would arrive and sometimes the children who lived next door to Granny and Grandad would come to play with him. They were girls aged three and four whose grandparents had come to Britain from Hong Kong. They gave Matthew some lovely silky, colourful clothes for his dressing-up box and sometimes their Daddy showed them all how to fly a kite. He was very good at it and had shown Matthew and his Grandad how to make a kite. They were all going kite-flying on the next windy day that they were free.

Gardening

Helping with the garden was a favourite activity. He would help to sow seeds and to plant out seedlings and was surprisingly adept at handling them. He would help to weed and ask endless questions about hoeing up potatoes and why the thermometer in the greenhouse had to be checked. Garden creatures fascinated him. He helped his Grandad to spread grit around some vegetables and flowers to prevent the slugs from destroying the plants. He took kitchen waste and put it in the compost bin and he helped to spread compost in the bean trench before planting the beans that had been grown from seed. Granny showed him how to dead-head the roses and even let him use her special tools under strict supervision. Together they planted some fast-growing sunflower seeds and in the winter-time he grew two amaryllis, one to take home and one to keep at Granny and Grandad's house.

From these activities Matthew learned more about the world, about co-operating with nature to enable plants to flourish, about times and seasons, about respecting and stewarding the earth. With conversation, more skills and the benefit of further experience, he will be able to care for his own plot of land and learn to think about great global and ethical issues facing human beings. His older cousin Amy was last seen wearing a T-shirt encouraging people to save the rain forests.

Library books, tapes and videos

Since their retirement Pat and Mike Johnston had used the library more than they had done during their paid work days. Once Matthew came to them regularly they discovered what a lot the library had to offer. Not only books but children's tapes (stories and music) and videos too. That was why a regular visit to the library was part of their routine. They would take Matthew and together they would choose what to borrow. Sometimes he would want to keep a favourite book for several weeks and that was all right. Hardly a day went by without them using something from the library. They would sing along to a tape, enjoy some action rhymes, read a story or listen to one on tape while following it in a book. Sometimes a tape would be borrowed that encouraged movement or dance. Matthew's grandparents were quite proud of the fact that he could listen and obey the instructions on the tapes. They were sure too that by using the library they were able to give him a wider variety of musical experiences than they could otherwise have done and he was able to choose books and videos that were appropriate to his age and ability as he grew.

112

Walks

Walks were always a favourite activity, partly because Granny and Grandad were good at making them fun. There was always something to look for or to count, whether it was the number of red vehicles that drove past them or the cracks in the pavement that had to be avoided. At different times of the year they would go on dandelion hunts, or chestnut hunts, or sticky bud hunts as a way of looking for signs of the different seasons. Sometimes they would take an urban walk and look for shapes (square, round and oblong windows), or different styles of architecture (pointed, flat, and sloping roofs), or the number of doors painted a certain colour. These walks increased Matthew's awareness of different environments (residential streets, shopping area, park, country, wet, dry, dull, sunny) and sensitized him to the seasons and the effects of the weather.

Of course, Pat and Mike were in a position to engage in a lot of activities with their grandson as designated child carers. Most grandparents do not have as much time with their grandchildren but most will have some opportunities when grandchildren visit, or when they visit their grandchildren, during school holidays or on shared holidays. The point is that, when grandparents are able, young grandchildren really appreciate the simplest of activities that do not require a lot of expensive resources. What they want are people who will interact with them, encourage them, join them in some activities and at other times invite the children to join them in their activities, often in a 'helping' capacity. When they do this they nurture their relationships with their grandchildren by sharing experiences and talking about them. Together they create important memories that both can take into the future with them.

A variety of activities undertaken in an encouraging environment is likely to enhance young children's self-esteem and to enable them to learn more about the world of which they are a part. When Matthew enters the reception class of his local school he will be ready to learn further because his many quality experiences of people, play and activities will have enabled the foundations for further learning to be in place. At this stage his grandparents will have to handle major changes in their days, which will have a different pattern to them without a grandchild in the house during school time.

Everyday activities with grandchildren

Having established a good relationship in early childhood, with some shared memories and interests, grandparents and grandchildren are likely to continue to value their special relationship. There will be adjustments in the relationship and in the activities that they enjoy together but the relationship is there.

Many of the activities that older children and teenagers enjoy are developments of those listed above — bicycle maintenance, barbecues, cooking, cake-decorating, chatting, camping, computers and the Internet, family history, fell-walking, photography, stamp-collecting, watching sport on television, playing board games, patchwork, crochet and knitting, watching videos, visiting art galleries or going to the theatre. (Perhaps the activities that older children enjoy with their grandparents are more expensive than those of younger children!) Sometimes activities may be undertaken separately, especially with older children/teenagers, but they form contact points, areas of shared interest that will be there through the rest of life. Most of all, however, grandchildren enjoy any activity that nurtures their special relationship with grandparents whom they have experienced as loving and life-affirming people.

'Nanny came to look after us'

Take Ten

* The types of activity that you do with your grandchildren will depend largely on their ages. List the names and ages of the children. Alongside each one write down some of the activities that that child has particularly enjoyed with you in the past. Make a note of a new activity that you might plan to do with that child, one that might capture interest and imagination and that you would both enjoy.

* Imagine that several grandchildren were coming together to your house. List some activities that might be appropriate to do with the group. Have a go.

A prayer of thanks

Thank you for simple things in life that I can do and share with grandchildren:

for their observations that help me to see the extraordinary in the ordinary;
for the shared moments of interest and insight;
for fun and laughter and, sometimes, tears;
for curiosity and questions;
and for the love that they give to me, their grandparent and elder.

Sharing values and beliefs with grandchildren

Sometimes grandparents wonder about the future of their grandchildren. How will they cope later in life? They know that times change and that there are pressures and influences on their grandchildren which could lead them into difficult territory so that they begin to live their lives by a set of values very different from those with which they were brought up. If the grandparents have a strong faith they wonder whether their grandchildren will share that faith. Mike and Pat Johnston were no exception. They belonged to the Christian tradition and had been active church members all their lives. As parents they had taken their three children to church regularly, prayed with them at home and generally encouraged them in the Christian faith, living in accordance with the values and beliefs of that faith as they understood them. Of course, there had been times when they fell short of their own standards, but they were human and they believed in a God who was gracious and forgiving. Even so, they had many lessons to learn as they brought up their offspring. One of them was that their children had to make their own way and they had to let them go to do that. There came a time when both Bob and Charlie chose not to share, or drifted away from, the faith of their parents though they still shared some of their values, e.g. racial equality. That does not mean that they will never share beliefs in the future, but at the moment they do not do so. Meanwhile their children, Pat and Mike's grandchildren, are being parented in a very materialistic world where consumerism is another name for the god of many people. There are times when Pat and Mike are concerned for the faith development of their grandchildren. Bob and Charlie know what their parents believe and respect them. On special occasions they will go to church with them — mainly out of respect for Pat and Mike — and they are not against their parents telling the grandchildren Bible stories or teaching them Christian songs. In that respect Pat and Mike are fortunate. In some families the atmosphere can be frosty between adult children and their parents when it comes to questions of faith. Much depends on the experiences that the adult children had of Christian people and churches and how their opting out of the faith community was handled. (Sometimes it can be the other way round, with the adult child opting into a faith community and the parents remaining outside it.)

Amy and Emma Foster are approaching the age when their Aunt Charlie began her teenage rebellion in style. It was at a similar age that their Uncle Bob slid away from the church. Pat and Mike wait to see what will happen with Emma and Amy. They are glad that the girls have a good relationship with their parents, Anne and David, and that all are actively involved in a church. The girls have been to several events and holidays with their peers in the church and they have a good set of friends there of all ages. It seems to Pat that they are well prepared and supported for the next stage of their life journey and she and Mike are there should they want to talk to their grandparents. In this uncertain world, though, Pat and Mike still wonder. What, if anything, can they do to nurture their grandchildren's faith development? Is it part of their role? It is a question that grandparents from traditions other than Christian also ask. While the content of their faiths may differ, how children are nurtured and enabled to hold a faith appears, from the research of James Fowler[1] and others[2], to be the same. Let me explain further.

In the last twenty years or so a good deal of research has been undertaken to help us to understand how faith grows in human beings, adults as well as children. The researchers have identified that there are stages of faith each with their own style. For instance, a child will have a child's style of faith while believing in the same thing or person — in the case of Christians, Jesus — as her parent who has an adult's style of faith (hopefully — not all adults reach a stage of mature faith). The researchers have concentrated on the process of faithing. At its simplest: we believe that a chair will hold us up so we act on that belief and sit on the chair but, say the researchers, how do we come to that belief and how do we go on believing? What is the process? Faith is active, something all human beings do. All give supreme worth to some god or gods; the god may be work, education, or career, or the house or family, or money, or a system of belief such as humanism or agnosticism or atheism, or Islam, or Sikhism, or the Christian God (the Father, Son and Spirit). As Fowler says, 'Our hearts inevitably rest somewhere', and people live and act according to their beliefs, but what is the process by which they came to hold them and how will that process continue? Briefly the process involves their experiences, affiliation to the faith of those closest to them, a period of searching for themselves and then coming to some conclusion of their own, deciding whether to follow the faith-way of parents, or of others they know, or neither.

In the rest of this chapter I shall confine myself to the faith development of children rather than the whole life-span because we are thinking particularly of grandchildren, and will comment from the perspective of my own faith background which is Christian.

John Westerhoff[3], who has worked in this field, identified four stages of faith in children and to help to make them clear he used the image of a tree. Imagine an acorn with its potential to grow into a massive oak tree, then the tiny seedling, then the sapling, and then the tree, growing year by year. Each year it adds a ring of wood to the tree trunk so that, should the trunk be sliced through, it would be possible to count the rings and know the age of the tree. The rings are not equal in thickness because each was affected by the growing conditions of the year in which it was formed. However, at each stage of its growth the tree is a complete tree. So babies and toddlers, school children and teenagers, young adults and old people are complete people who may share a faith but they will hold it differently.

Experienced faith

Let us begin with the centre ring, which Westerhoff calls a period of *experienced faith* when the experiences of being loved and cared for are vital. The young baby feels secure in the parent's arms. Needs are met. The child feels comfortable or secure and safe — the carers are trustworthy. A sense of security begins to develop. Through the rough and tumble of daily living in the home, youngsters experience love, justice, fairness, forgiveness, joy, sorrow, etc. To them their carers (the significant adults in their lives) are the source of all knowledge and authority. They are the ones they love and who enable them to flourish (or otherwise). In the early years these close and significant adults are pictures of God to their children; some have said that they are 'living icons' and Fowler suggested that God is mediated 'through recognizing eyes and confirming smiles'.

It follows that children in loving families, whatever the shape of the family, are going to have positive experiences that will inform their early pictures of God. Through experience they are coming face to face with what, as they will later be taught, Christians believe to be the attributes of God — God is love, all-knowing, just, forgiving, gracious, etc. Take Matthew Foster, for instance. By the age of two-ish he knew that there were some boundaries to be kept and his understanding of boundaries and boundary-keeping has been developing through experience ever since. When he breaks boundaries then he understands his sources of authority; in his case his Mum or grandparents, who are displeased, hurt and angry, and so Matthew experiences the consequences of his boundary breaking, i.e. the displeasure of his Mum or grandparents. He also experiences their forgiveness and grace. They are reconciled and the displeasure does not last for long because he is sorry and he is the apple of their eye. They forgive and delight in him. Young children feel and experience these things and when they do so they experience faith in action. As they grow and hear more of the content of the faith then it resonates with their experience.

In his early years Matthew Johnston has experienced the attitudes of his sources of authority (Mum and grandparents) to the world and to its Maker. In his case he has observed much of the natural world, its beauty, pattern, rhythm, and has experienced caring for it or stewarding it with his grandparents. You could say that helping to make compost or taking the newspapers to the recycling bin or being trained never to drop litter are experiences that have influenced the process of Matthew's faith development. They are activities that are rooted in his grandparents' belief that the earth is the Lord's and they are to help to care for it. (It is also true that other people may care for the earth for different reasons.) Similarly, experiences of Mum and grandparents' creativity and of their affirmation of his creative activities, e.g. junk modelling, painting, or creative behaviour, are experiences that help him to know that creativity is a good thing and something that they value. As the content of their faith becomes clearer to him, he will also understand that Christians believe that human creativity is part of the image of God that they bear, and that his grandparents' values about creativity spring from that belief.

However, it may be a while before those connections are made. For the moment the experience is sufficient.

Young children observe and imitate those close to them. They are conditioned through rewards and punishments so they will be kind because they like the pleasurable reward of praise or a hug from their parents when they are kind or generous or caring. They want to do what they see their significant adults do and to find out more about the world, so they play out situations. They become Mummy or Daddy in their play and sometimes, if prayer or church is a part of their lives, they will play churches too. Play experiences can be important at this stage of faith development. They are another type of experience that leaves children with what Fowler calls 'a chaos of powerful images' derived from experiences and stories. Early childhood is a period when children build up all kinds of impressions of the world that God has made and these impressions will be sorted out into some order during the next phase or stage of faith development.

Before moving to the next phase, however, let us pause to think about some of the implications of this first stage of faith for grandparents. First we must recognize that, whether they like it or not, parents and all who are significant in the lives of young children are affecting their faith development through the everyday experiences of family life that they share with them. They are being observed and copied and through shared experiences they are leaving children with many powerful images — images of warmth, love, care, kindness, fun, responsibility, trust, sadness, friendship, creativity. In fact they are pictures of their God to their children. Wow! (The contrary may also be possible in an unloving home where there may be hate, unkindness and, in the worst cases, abuse.) The primary carers of young children, usually the parents, are the biggest influence here and they need all the support and encouragement that they can get to provide a warm, loving, consistent and trusting environment for children. In such an environment children will flourish and the foundations for holding faith will be laid. So whatever grandparents might do to encourage their adult children and to support them as parents will indirectly affect the faith development of their grandchildren. Poverty, poor housing, sleep deprivation, illness, unemployment and poor communication skills all contribute to making the task of parenting more difficult and affect the quality of the experiences that children are likely to have.

Pat and Mike Johnston were able to play a big part in Matthew's development because they were engaged in a lot of caring. Their part in their granddaughter Chloe's development is less so but it does not mean that it is insignificant. When she visits, or they visit her, they can still ensure that she has good experiences, that they are warm and loving, accepting and forgiving, that she feels listened to and affirmed, that she has fun with them and joins them in activities. Through their choice of gifts at Christmas and birthdays they can reflect values that are consistent with their faith, e.g. black dolls and white dolls, boy dolls and girl dolls. In this way they contribute to the chaos of images that Fowler described and that she will sort out in her thinking as she grows. Continued interest and a warm relationship can also be nurtured down the telephone line. While the experience of a good relationship is invaluable at all stages of life, it is especially so in the phase of experienced faith. You may not have so much time with your grandchildren but what is important is that your grandchildren have a good experience of you, know that they are loved by you and value their relationship with you. Such an experience of a person who mediates God to children will leave them with some impressions of what God is like.

Take Ten

Reflect on some of the experiences you have had with young grandchildren or other young children.

* What are the values that underpin what you have done with them?

* What impressions or images of you (good and bad) might the children have formed as a result of these experiences with and of you?

* Of these impressions, which do you think reflect the image of God in you and which reflect the fallen side of your human nature? Children will pick up both from you — that's life.

At this stage the two types of impressions that children may have gleaned from you and their parent/carers are part of the chaos of impressions. At a later stage, they will have to sort out the chaos and recognize that significant adults make mistakes and are not, in fact, God. That is an important piece of learning — parents and grandparents are not all-knowing. I can remember feeling really let down by my Dad when I first recognized and admitted to myself that he was wrong about something.

Affiliative faith

The second ring in our tree is described by Westerhoff as *affiliative faith*. It is a time when the children's world expands and more people join with the significant adults in their lives as authority figures — teachers, church group leaders, club leaders and, I suppose, some of the influential people who appear on television. Friends become more important too. It is obvious then that there may be influential figures in children's lives who are communicating different values and beliefs. However, at this stage children affiliate to, or attach themselves to, the faith of their closest significant adults, usually that of family members. If they value the Christian story the children will, if they pray children will, and if other adults believe the same, well, that is a bonus. At this stage children sort out fantasy from what is true or real though they still think concretely. It is a stage of making sense out of the impressions that they have. Stories are of special interest so the stories of the faith can be important at this stage and so is 'my story' or 'our story'. It is a good time to explore the family story and to tell and show it using photographs of some of the important events in your earlier years and the parents'.

Bob Johnston's stepson Jamie is in a stage of affiliative faith. He spends time between the homes of his mother Ishbel and his birth-father and experiences two ways of being family. In addition he is still in touch with grandparents and that is good. During the period of upheaval, while his parents were going through the breakdown of their marriage, his grandparents became even more special, at least one set did while the other was unsure about how to handle the situation. Now Jamie is quite used to spending a weekend with his Dad at his grandparents' home. Once Bob married Ishbel, Jamie also gained a set of step-grandparents, Pat and Mike, who were kind and welcoming. His new 'cousin' Matthew loved these grandparents and sometimes he and Jamie played together at their house. He soon learned that he was loved by his new step-grandparents. It is clear that Jamie grew through his stage of experienced faith, finding some of his experiences painful and negative, but the adults in his life have co-operated to let him know that he is well loved and cared for. (Let us be clear that all children will have some painful experiences to handle.) So Jamie entered the affiliative stage of faith with a range of good and bad memories and impressions. In sorting them out and being enabled to grow he has needed to be given constant reassurance and affirmation, to have fun doing ordinary things and to learn to laugh and trust again. Now he is working on his story with various grandparents and is aware that households are different. There are some values that his parents, grandparents and stepfamily share and they are the ones that speak loudest to him — not that he has identified this for himself. He likes stories, especially stories where good triumphs over evil, because fairness and justice are important to him. He is extremely sensitive to what he perceives to be fair or unfair actions, particularly those of the significant adults in his life like his teachers. This is a good time to speak of a God of justice. When he is with his birth-father's family, he generally goes along with their ways of doing things, and when he is with his mother's family he goes along with them.

Searching faith

Westerhoff calls the third ring in the tree trunk a period of *searching faith*. By this time children have acquired more sophisticated language, thinking and reasoning skills. They begin to ask questions and perhaps doubt what those closest to them believe. At the stage of affiliative faith, children believe because people who are significant to them believe, but in the period of searching faith there are sometimes doubts, especially if their peers believe something else. In other words it is at this stage that children want to test out their earlier beliefs against the beliefs of others, e.g. friends and peer group, and to find some answers for themselves. It is a stage when they commit to causes and to people. The 'in group' is important and self-awareness increases as youngsters approach puberty.

Amy and Emma Foster have reached this stage of faith. While they question the values and beliefs of their parents, they are enabled to do so by members of their extended faith community who have become mentors and friends. They are fortunate because they belong to a church where, as children, they were included in its community life and so they know people of all ages and have a sense of belonging. It is at this stage that many youngsters begin to slip away from church, often because they do not feel part of the whole community and do not have a safe environment within it in which to ask their questions and to explore them honestly without receiving prescriptive answers. At this stage parents are not always the easiest people with whom to explore values and beliefs because the youngsters are basically challenging them and this is where grandparents may again find that they have a special role to play. Their grandchildren, in this phase of faith development, may choose to talk to them, to ask questions. When this happens, take it as a compliment. You have obviously established and sustained a meaningful relationship with your grandchild.

Sometimes youngsters in this stage need to take time to explore completely away from close relatives. They require space in which to doubt, and doubt is healthy. They also need to critique the faith of their parents and to explore their faith questions. Eventually, however, most will come to the next phase of faith development.

Owned faith

Westerhoff's fourth ring represents the time when people say, 'This is what I believe. I believe it, not because my parents or close relatives or mentors do, but because I have chosen to believe. I place my faith in ... and will live my life in accordance with these beliefs.' Of course, the person making this statement might have chosen to own a faith with content different from that of those who were significant in earlier years. That is their choice and it must be respected.

I remember a young person of fourteen coming home from a youth camp where she had been with friends and some mentors. On arrival she told us with excitement that she had become a Christian. It was a great day for her and we were all thrilled. Afterwards I reflected on her statement and realized that she might have said, 'I have owned my Christian faith for myself.' I remembered her saying with real feeling when she was three years old, 'I really love Jesus'. That was when she held her faith as a three-year-old. Later there were signs of affiliation when she believed in Jesus because family members did, and then there was a time of thinking things out for herself, of asking questions of one or two mentors and deciding to believe and live her life according to the values of her faith. She had come to a point of owning what she believed and she experienced it as the event when she became a Christian. I saw it as part of a process of faith development because she loved Jesus at three and eight and ten — she just held her faith differently in ways appropriate to her age and maturation. As Fowler has written, 'One who becomes Christian in childhood may indeed remain Christian all of his or her life. But one's WAY of being Christian will need to deepen, expand and be reconstituted several times in the pilgrimage of faith.'

Through this process of faithing, grandparents can be alongside in various roles — as intercessors, as role-models, as listeners and advisers, as mentors (sometimes to grandchildren and sometimes to their parents). Grandparents can be ready to chat about their beliefs and values in discussions and when asked to do so. However, primarily, their faith and the attitudes and values that are important to them will be communicated as they relate to grandchildren, as they share experiences and play with them, and as they respond in awe and wonder to what God has made and done. Their attitudes to their grandchildren will be important in this — they must respect them and keep confidences, encourage them to explore their own questions of faith rather than the grandparents', and genuinely enable them to explore rather than receive prescribed answers, while being ready to express an opinion if asked.

Take Ten

* ✱ Having read this chapter note down any questions that it raises for you.
* ✱ You might pursue your questions using some of the books referred to in the resources list.
* ✱ Consider your grandchildren, or children you know. Where do you see them as being in the process of faith development? You might see the same child in several places at the same time. That is all right. The stages described are a general rule and there will be exceptions to it. How best might you contribute to the nurture of their faith development?

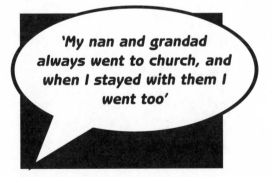

'My nan and grandad always went to church, and when I stayed with them I went too'

Prayer

Lord, you said, 'Let the children come to me.'
It was a shock for those around you who would
have kept them away — because they were only
children.

Help me to encourage them in their coming:
by loving them;
by helping them to see and appreciate what you
have made;
by sharing my life with them;
by being ready to listen, to tell stories and to pray;
by exploring their questions with them;
and by being ready to share the story of my faith.

References

1 Fowler J, *Stages of Faith* (Dove Communications 1981).

2 Dykstra C and Parks S, *Faith Development and Fowler* (Religious Education Press, Alabama 1986).

3 Westerhoff J, *Will Our Children Have Faith?* (Seabury Press 1976).

For further reading:
How Faith Grows (The National Society and Church House Publishing 1991).

Listening to grandchildren

When Jamie, Pat and Mike Johnston's step-grandson, joined their extended family he was quite young. He had not started full-time education but was used to child care, his mother having a full-time job. There had been a lot of change in Jamie's life. He had lived through the break-up of his parents' marriage, he had lived alone with his mother for a few months and then got to know a strange man whom his mum spent a lot of time with. Then Jamie and his mum moved to live in a big house with this man, who was called Bob and who was to be his stepdad. Jamie was not sure what a stepdad was. It was all very confusing but his stepdad was probably going to be OK. He liked kicking a ball around with Jamie though he was not at home a great deal during the week. Life took on a new pattern for Jamie — one weekend with his birth-father and then one with his mum and stepdad. There had been so much change in his short life and Jamie had developed some coping strategies because he had had to handle so many new situations and a whole melting pot of emotions. If asked how he was he could not have identified his feelings, partly because he did not have the emotional language and partly because he did not know the answer to the question. Sometimes Jamie pretended not to hear and often he was quiet, playing with small toys in an imaginary world, then at other times he would kick a ball around as fiercely as he could. When he first met his new step-grandparents he was rather wary of them and stuck close to his mum.

Pat and Mike wondered how they were going to get on with their new step-grandson. For them it was a new situation and there was a lot going on in their lives. They were supporting Charlie with her young baby, Matthew, at the time. They knew that they would see Jamie less

127

often than they would see their other grandchildren because he spent time with his birth-father regularly and Bob and Ishbel worked long hours during the week. As they thought about Jamie they realized he had been through a lot of change and felt that he was probably a troubled young boy with low self-esteem. How could they help him?

They decided that they would treat him as much as possible like their other grandchildren and that meant that they would build a relationship with him, and take an interest in him and in what he was doing. They would love him and they began by listening, not to spoken words but to the non-verbal communication that came from Jamie through his behaviour. They noticed his coping strategies, his interests and his wariness of new people. What might he be saying? One of the things that he was saying to Pat and Mike was, 'I have had so much change in my life that I do not know if I can trust you.'

There is probably nothing more significant that a person can do to build self-esteem than to listen. Listening itself is a form of non-verbal communication. Through it we say, 'You are worth listening to,' and the receiver of our non-verbal message concludes, 'She thinks I have value. She respects me.' So one of the important communication tasks for grandparents wanting to build relationships and to listen is to do what Michael Quinn[1] calls 'Read the signals.' Children have feelings; even those who have not experienced the amount of change that Jamie had experienced have feelings, and until adults can read the signs they find it difficult to know how a child feels, or to understand or to appreciate and support them. From Jamie's initial non-verbal communication Pat and Mike discerned a lot that would help them as they spent more time with him. Mike made sure that there was a decent football at their house — they would begin with an obvious interest — and Pat had pastry available for making jam tarts. In her experience it was quite a calming medium with which to work and often children would begin to chat while they worked alongside each other with the pastry.

How many times have you been asked, 'How are you?' and replied, 'All right', when you have a thumping headache, have been awake most of the night and have lost the family cat? A discerning person will read your body language or listen to your non-verbal communication and conclude that there is a gap between your real feeling and what you have said. In the UK we are not good at talking about feelings, yet we all have them, both good and bad feelings. Sometimes we need to own them and to talk about them. When someone discerns what is going on inside us we feel understood and affirmed. So taking time, as Pat and Mike did, to notice and be sensitive to Jamie's behaviour helped them to understand what was going on inside him and to create opportunities for him to talk during the course of normal play and activities. Pat and Mike also noticed that Jamie was already coming to terms with some of his confusions through his own play and they would encourage that by making sure there was suitable equipment to hand.

Non-verbal communication, therefore, gives good clues that reveal how a person is feeling. We all use it and would be wise to recognize it when we see it. Look for eye contact, facial expression (smile, sympathy, pain, raised eye-brows), the nodding of the head in agreement or understanding, body posture, appropriate touch and how far apart people are sitting or standing. With children, also look for big arm movements and energetic activity, or unusual quietness, or withdrawal or moodiness as they get older. All such behaviours are signs of inner activity.

The second form of listening that grandparents might use is perhaps the one that is more obvious. It is verbal communication. Listen to the words and especially to the tone of the words.

'Mum's mum talks a lot, just like our mum'

Take Ten

Sit in front of a mirror and make these facial expressions — happy, angry, frightened, and sad. Now say the words, 'I think you are fantastic,' four times, each time with a different facial expression and tone of voice, i.e. happy, angry, frightened, sad.

The words may remain the same but the meaning is different. Good listeners listen for the true meaning of what is being said.

Listening to grandchildren

When grandparents listen they teach their grandchildren to listen in turn. It also enables them to talk. As Michael Quinn says, 'Listening heals, it teaches children to respect themselves and others, and it helps them to be self-confident and happy.' Effective listening involves genuinely caring and wanting to understand the child; remaining quiet but letting the child know that you are listening by nodding the head or saying 'Mmm' at appropriate times, and keeping eye contact. (In some play or activity situations children and young people may talk while being busy with their hands and then sustained eye contact may not be possible.) Expressing your response in your eyes and being relaxed while not invading the speaker's space is important too. So is the encouragement to go on speaking because for most children their greatest need is to talk, to express their thoughts, feelings and whatever else is going on inside them. Beware of questions and giving advice because they can close children up before they have talked enough and can make them feel worse.

There is a form of listening called *active listening* which many parents and grandparents are learning to use. With active listening the listener tries to understand what the speaker is really feeling and then plays it back to the speaker. For instance, when Jamie was about to begin school he said to Pat, 'I don't want to go to school.' She could have said to him something like, 'Oh it'll be all right,' or ' Don't be silly. School's fun.' Both those responses are answers that I have heard but neither would be appropriate because it is obvious that Jamie is unsure about going into a new situation and is apprehensive. To say these things would deny his feelings and could make him feel that he is wrong to feel as he does. Therefore Pat's response was, 'It sounds as if you're feeling that you don't know what school will be like and you're a bit scared?' In other words, she reflected to Jamie what he was feeling and let him know that she understood how he was feeling. This approach also gave him the opportunity to talk more about his feelings should he choose to do so. Active listening is particularly helpful to children, especially when they have experienced trauma or loss and are feeling things deeply.

In order to listen actively grandparents need to decide to do so because they care. At first, responding to children in this way may feel strange and grandparents may need a little time to get used to it but it will be worth it because listening in this way works. Always listen for the feelings behind the words. As a young teacher I remember the same question coming from children day after day. It was, 'Please may

130

I go to the toilet?' Listening for the feelings behind the question helped me to understand the children and what they were feeling. Some were really feeling that they needed a break from their maths, some were feeling that they wanted to chat with friends, some genuinely wanted and needed to visit the toilets and occasionally some were feeling ill. The message could be, 'I've lost interest and feel bored', or 'I feel the need to relieve myself,' or 'I feel unwell' and these were the feelings/messages to be played back to the children as appropriate.

Active listeners reflect the feelings behind the words to their grandchildren

By deciding to listen to Jamie, Pat and Mike helped him through some difficult times. He was encouraged and affirmed and his self-esteem began to develop.

As I said earlier, listening becomes important during times of loss or grief. Of course we grow up experiencing minor losses and receive some training for the major losses as we handle the losing of a tooth, or a toy, or a pet. When more severe loss occurs, e.g. through separation, divorce or death, then a range of feelings will be experienced by the children. In many families, however, the emotional support is given to the closest adults, e.g. the spouse of the deceased or the parent of a dead child, but children have feelings too and they grieve, though they may express their grief differently at different stages of understanding and development. At such times those who might normally support them are handling their own grief and in no position to help children. Warm, caring people who can listen actively and understand what the children are feeling are needed to support them through such a period of their lives.

It is now some years since Jamie joined Pat and Mike Johnston's extended family. He is now a well integrated member of it. He has come to love his step-grandparents and he knows that they love and understand him because they listen.

Take Ten

Practise some active listening.

Decide what you would say to show that you understand the feelings:

* ✳ It's not fair. I never get picked for the football team.
* ✳ Other people stay up to watch the television. Why can't I?
* ✳ I'm rubbish. I got hardly any of my spellings right.
* ✳ Guess what! Jenny has invited me to her birthday party.

Prayer

Lord,

Thank you for listening and understanding how I feel.

Help me to listen to my grandchildren. Through my listening may they —

feel valued and encouraged,

feel understood,

and like themselves more

because they are fearfully and wonderfully made.

Reference

1 Quinn M and T, *What Can a Parent Do?* (Family Caring Trust 1986).

When the unthinkable happens

A grandmother shared her story with others on a course called *Surviving Secrets*. This is what she said.

'Five years ago I was looking after my grandsons. We were watching TV when one of them told me, "Grandma, my Daddy does something to me I don't like." My heart sank, so I told him to say, "No". He said, "I do, Grandma."

'My grandson, Tom, had been withdrawn and tearful for some time. We thought it would be something he would grow out of. This couldn't be happening to my grandchildren — we were a "normal family". I was thankful that my grandson was able to tell me and trust me. It was hard to tell my daughter.

'She left her husband and she and the children came to live with me. She did not know where to go for help and advice but decided to go to the Citizen's Advice Bureau. My daughter then informed the Police and Social Workers. When the Police interviewed the children, Tom, the younger child, just counted five times on his fingers. Michael aged six, would not say anything happened to him, but the Police believed he, too, had been sexually abused. I cannot write down in words how relieved I felt that Tom had told someone else as well as me. After all this time Tom still cannot talk to his Mum about it.

'Michael is now aged eleven and still suffers. He is a very sad, very unhappy boy. He is seeing an Educational Psychologist and is having art therapy to help him to talk about the abuse. He soils his pants every day, so he smells. He "comfort eats" and is getting so overweight he cannot play football, the sport

*he loves. He also has eczema and scratches his skin until it
bleeds. He seems to want to punish himself all the time.*

*'My daughter blames herself for not being aware of the abuse.
Sometimes I feel so helpless and ask, "What has happened to my
family?" Sometimes I wonder where God is to children who
suffer so. If it was not for the Support Group of a church in a
nearby town I don't know what I would do. We meet every three
weeks to talk about our problems and pray for each other. No
one in my church understands or wants to help. The only
response I get is, "It does not happen in our church".'*

Unfortunately sexual abuse occurs in 'normal' families and is
common to all classes, races, religions and locations. Most abusers
live perfectly respectable lives. Ninety per cent are known to the
children they abuse and are often members of their own families.
Abusers are usually heterosexual men but information from the USA
suggests that increasingly children are disclosing that women abused
them. According to research done for the BBC and quoted in the
Surviving Secrets handouts, approximately ten per cent of the
general population in Britain were abused as children, twelve per cent
of females and eight per cent of males. While the average age for
abuse to start is eight years five months in girls, it is eight years seven
months in boys, though they generally wait until they are twelve plus
before disclosing the abuse.

What is meant by the term 'sexual abuse'? A definition used at the
Surviving Secrets course is:

*'Sexual abuse occurs when another person who is in a position
of greater power than the victim exposes the victim to any of
the following: sexual intercourse (anal, oral, vaginal); sexual
touching; exposure of the sexual organs; showing pornographic
material or talking about things in an erotic way.'*

The 'greater power' referred to is by virtue of age, emotional maturity,
gender, intellect or physical strength. With this definition in mind let
us remember that a 'one-off' incident may have as profound an effect
on one child as repeated abuse has on another.

A child who has suffered from sexual abuse may well find the easiest
person to disclose the abuse to is a grandparent or someone who is
not as close as 'the other parent.' The nature of the relationship
makes this so, often because grandparents provide a caring, receptive
environment so the child feels safe enough to disclose the secret that

may have been kept for a long time. On reflection Tom's grandma realized that there were signs of Tom's unhappiness before his disclosure. He had been withdrawn and tearful. Now, not every child who is withdrawn and tearful is suffering from sexual abuse. There could be a whole range of reasons for the behaviour such as sickness, bullying at school, parental conflict, or loss of a friendship. It is important, therefore, not to jump to conclusions but to recognize when such behaviour is observed that the child is troubled and may need to talk. However, it is the child's choice whether to talk, even in the face of strong suspicions of abuse. Grandparents, or others, have the role of loving the child, of maintaining a caring relationship with a history of listening and respect, so that the child can choose to talk. It is not the grandparent's role to force grandchildren to talk to them.

All sorts of behavioural, physical or medical signs may indicate that a child is troubled and grandparents are often in a good position to observe them. Again the generation gap sometimes helps them to 'see the wood for the trees' in a way that a parent or parents cannot do so easily because they are too close. So watch out for sudden changes in behaviour such as falling standards in schoolwork, inability to concentrate, sleeplessness, fear of the dark, depression, bed-wetting, recurring urinary tract infections, venereal disease, reluctance to be with certain people or displays of sexual knowledge beyond their years — even in drawings. Some children and young people might begin to steal, play truant, experiment with drugs and alcohol, or withdraw from family and friends. Such behaviours are sad but eloquent ways in which a child might communicate the message, 'I am troubled and hurting'. Once more I must emphasize that there is a range of reasons why a child might be troubled and hurting, so avoid jumping to conclusions about the cause and if at all possible sensitively create opportunities for children to talk should they wish to do so. At this stage they need support and help in adjusting behaviour that may be understandable while being unacceptable.

If grandchildren do decide to talk and disclose abuse, or if you have good reason to suspect abuse, act quickly. Listen carefully, keep calm and look. Accept what they say and do not promise confidentiality. Instead let them know that you will have to tell someone. Do not push for more information than is offered but reassure the children that they were right to tell you and you believe them. Remember that they may be scared because they may have broken a promise of secrecy or have been threatened by the abuser. Keep them informed of what you are going to do next and promise to let them know what happens. Make detailed notes of what was said, record dates and times and keep handwritten records. Then follow a pattern similar to the one that Tom's grandma took, i.e. tell the other parent and ensure that the statutory services responsible for child protection are informed. This can be done through the Social Services Department that has the main responsibility for children at risk, or through the National Society for the Prevention of Cruelty to Children, or the police. In all authorities these groups have procedures to follow in cases of suspected child abuse. It may be that a grandparent will be invited to a Case Conference carried out by social workers and police. If so, the grandparent needs to know the role to take. In other words, is the invitation to go along as a support to the child or is it to give information?

Prompt action may be taken to remove the abuser from the family home and to deny that person access to the child. Again there will be a whole range of feelings experienced by different members of the family. One parent may feel totally betrayed by a partner and devastated that she (it is usually the mother) has not noticed her partner's behaviour, rather like Tom's mother. Another parent may enter complete denial of the situation or just become numb initially. In many ways the abused child may think that the abuser's behaviour was normal and may still love that person, probably Dad, an older brother or relative, and again the child may be upset because there is no access, for safety reasons, to the person who is still loved. In the midst of this dynamic will be other family members, including grandparents, who may become a major source of support for the remaining parent and child(ren).

At this point too it is worth sparing a thought for those grandparents who discover that it is their adult son or daughter who is the abuser. They will be in need of support themselves as they come to terms with the reality that it is their child who has acted in such a way towards their grandchildren. One of the hardest things for many of them is that they may lose contact with their grandchildren. There are agencies that may be able to provide help and support to such families. Please see the resources section of this book.

Whatever the cause of children's troubled thoughts and emotional hurting, their self-image is likely to be affected. They may feel unnecessarily guilty or ashamed through no fault of their own. This is especially true of victims of child sexual abuse who often feel dirty, bad and used. Sometimes children feel unlovable, worthless and unable to trust others because they have been so badly let down. Again, for the victim of sexual abuse, there may be questions about love and whether it is the same as sex, there may be feelings of helplessness and of everything being out of control. Depression is not uncommon and a range of turbulent feelings may be experienced at the same time — fear, anger, loss, and confusion. With all of this happening it is no wonder that so many children learn to dislike themselves and their bodies and that many who have kept a hidden secret for a long time become silent and withdrawn people, often isolated from other relationships. When this happens, children sometimes need specialist help and so do parents. At this point some grandparents are able to support by finding out where help may be available and ensuring that it is obtained.

'What has happened to my family?'

Whatever happens, the road to wholeness, after abuse, is long and painful not only for the child but for parents, siblings and other relatives, but it is worth taking. Grandparents who are able might keep in touch, offer encouragement and support, perhaps help financially and of course pray. They too might recognize their own need for support and look for it just as Tom's grandmother did.

Take Ten

Imagine that Tom's family, including his grandmother, lives in your street. In what ways might the neighbours and friends support them? If you were the grandmother in this family, whom might you turn to for support? What might a local church or faith community do to help and support while co-operating with local authority services?

A prayer for abused grandchildren

Imagine...

a young innocent child with lively blue eyes ... a child who laughs a lot ... a child with pink, glowing cheeks who runs and skips and dances...

Enter an adult, a familiar person with a cold smile on his face — the smile is unreal ... he has his way.

The child screams ... there is fear in her eyes ... she no longer skips and dances. Instead she feels guilty ... she cries sometimes with no tears ... the emotional scars run deep ... whom can she trust?

Pray
for this child and others like her. Pray that she may find love and gentleness, understanding and acceptance, healing and compassion as she slowly, slowly, very slowly reaches out to her Maker and learns to trust and dance again.

Reference

Surviving Secrets was a course organized by the Diocese of Southwell. Tom's story is reprinted with permission, and further information has been taken from the course handouts.

The adventure continues

The celebration for Pat and Mike Johnston's fortieth wedding anniversary was a great success. Everyone enjoyed it, not least their grandchildren who were all present. Watching the youngsters having fun added to Pat and Mike's pleasure. They appreciated their grandchildren, and were grateful for the new lease of life that they had given them when young and for the way in which having the children around enriched their lives. When Mike had retired they had had to make choices. With more free time and all the options available to active people after they have retired from paid employment, they could have chosen to be free from regular commitments with grandchildren, especially Matthew's child care. They could have blown their life savings on travel and on themselves. Instead they chose to put their major investment into their relationships with their grandchildren and to support their children by doing this. It does not mean that they subsumed themselves in the lives of these children. In fact they developed their individual and shared interests, and continued with their church activities, their friends and the occasional holiday without any members of the family joining them.

Watching their grandchildren, unique and special, they were glad that they had invested time and energy in them in different ways. It had not always been easy and there had been unexpected twists and turns along the way. Sometimes it had been hard to keep quiet when they might have handled a situation differently from their children. They were glad that they had always managed to keep the channels of communication open, having aimed to co-operate with their children rather than tell them what to do. In return they had been given the opportunity to share their lives with the next-but-one generation of their family.

The adventure continues

Through the Ruby Wedding party they were given a glimpse of how much they were loved and appreciated. There were several points when Pat felt a lump rise up in her throat.

Jamie had given her and Mike a card that he had made with a bunch of red tissue paper flowers on the front and the words, 'Red flowers for a Ruby Wedding' written on it. Inside he had written, 'I would give you a bunch of red flowers every day if I could.' Matthew had put so many kisses on his card that there was hardly room for his name and Ishbel had called her 'Mum' for the first time.

As for their children — Anne, Bob and Charlie?

They were grateful for the spirit of co-operation that they felt they had with Pat and Mike.

They were glad that when they might have said, 'In my day we did it this way', or 'Try doing...', Pat and Mike had learned to bite their tongues (most of the time anyway).

They were pleased that their parents were approachable and would talk about things.

They were glad that their children had grandparents whom they loved and had fun with.

They were grateful that their parents had time for the children, played with them and stimulated them to learn.

They were glad their parents were good, honest, wise people who would be there when needed.

It was time for the toasts. 'Here's to the future.' Yes, Pat and Mike had achieved forty years together and fifteen of them as grandparents, but who knows? They may have another twenty or more years together and throughout that time they will be continuing to grandparent their grandchildren into adulthood. Their adventure continues and so might yours.

'I'd like to give my Nan a hug every day'

Resources

Useful resources for parents and others

Birth to Five: A guide to the first five years of being a parent. From the Health Education Authority, Hamilton House, Mabledon Place, London WC1H 9TX

Care for the Family: Produces resources on parenting. From Garth House, Leon Avenue, Cardiff CF4 7RG

Everyday Problems in Childhood: An open learning course for parents of young children, with discussion materials on temper tantrums, aggression, sleep problems, eating, dressing, going out, separation. From The Parent Company, PO Box 1005, Brighton, BN1 3NA

Family Caring Trust: A series of group materials for parents that also might be used by grandparents and carers. Includes books, tapes, videos on Basic Parenting, Noughts to Sixes Parenting, Teen Parenting, Parenting and Sex. From 44 Rathfriland Road, Newry, Co Down, BT34 1LD

Positive Parenting — raising children with self-esteem: A book by Elizabeth Hartley Brewer (1994) to empower and encourage parents focusing on confidence building, self-esteem and self-reliance. Materials for group leaders and parent groups. From Cedar Books, Michelin House, 81 Fulham Road, London SW3 6RB

Teenagers in the Family: A series of tapes about teenagers under stress, sexuality, drugs. From The Trust for the Study of Adolescence, 23 New Road, Brighton, East Sussex, BN1 1WZ. Also available from them is the *Really Helpful Directory: services for pregnant teenagers and young parents.*

Some useful addresses

Care for the Family
Garth House, Leon Avenue, Cardiff CF4 7RG.

Children Need Grandparents
2 Surrey Way, Laindon West, Basildon, Essex SS15 6PS.
Tel: 01268 414607.
Offers mutual aid and advice to grandparents who are refused access to their grandchildren.

The Children's Society
Edward Rudolf House, Margery Street, London WC1X OJL.
Tel: 0171 837 4299

Churches Together for Families
c/o The Free Churches' Council (Pauline Butcher),
27 Tavistock Square, London WC1H 9HH.
Tel: 0171 387 8413

The Lord Chancellor's Department
81 Chancery Lane, London WC2 1DD.
Tel: 0171 911 7047

Families Anonymous
A self-help group for families of drug users with branches in different parts of the UK. Tel: 0171 498 4680.

Family Action Information and Rescue
PO Box 12, London WC1N 3XX.
Tel: 0181 539 3940. Helpline: 01482 443104
Advice for families with young people in extreme religious cults.

Family Caring Trust
44 Rathfriland Road, Newry, Co Down, BT34 1LD.

Families Need Fathers
134 Curtain Road, London EC2A 3AR.
 Tel: 0181 886 0970.
Advice and support for separating and divorcing parents to ensure their children remain in contact (including unmarried parents).

Family Rights Group
The Print House, 18 Ashwin Street, London E8 3DL.
Tel: 0171 923 2628

Family Life and Marriage Education
Robert Runcie House, 60 Marsham St, Maidstone, Kent ME14 1EW.
Tel: 01662 755014

Grandparents' Federation
Moot House, The Stowe, Harlow, Essex CM20 3AG.
Tel: 01279 444964

Mothers' Union
Mary Sumner House, 24 Tufton Street, London SW1P 3RB.
Tel: 0171 222 5533

National Christian Education Council
1020 Bristol Road, Selly Oak, Birmingham, B29 6LB.
Tel: 0121 472 4242

National Council for One-parent Families
255 Kentish Town Road, London NW5 2LX.
Tel: 0171 267 1361

National Society for the Prevention of Cruelty to Children
42 Curtain Road, London EC2A 3NH.
Emergency Helpline: 0800 800 500

National Stepfamily Association
3rd Floor, Chapel House, 18 Hatton Place, London EC1N 8RU.
Tel: 0171 209 2464.

NCH Action for Children
85 Highbury Park, London N5 1UD.
Tel: 0171 226 2033.

Parent Network
44-46 Caversham Road, London NW5 DDS

Pre-school Learning Alliance
69 Kings Cross Road, London WC1X 9LL.
Tel: 0171 833 0991

Reunite National Council for Abducted Children
Box 4, London WC1X 3DX.
Tel: 0171 404 8356

Royal Association for Disability and Rehabilitation
12 City Forum, 250 City Road, London EC1V 8AF.
Tel: 0171 250 3222.

Royal National Institute for the Blind
224 Great Portland Street, London W1N 6AA.
Tel: 0171 388 1266.

Royal National Institute for Deaf People
105 Gower Street, London WC1E 6AH.
Tel: 0171 387 8033.

FAITH *in* THE FUTURE

An initiative to meet the challenges of being Christian in today's and tomorrow's world

The *Faith in the Future* project has been developed by the National Christian Education Council to meet these current challenges:

∗ **How** can Christians make a vital contribution to the world of the young?

∗ **How** does our Christian faith inform the values we hold and the attitudes we adopt, and how do they make a difference to the people around us and the children in our care?

∗ **How** do we listen and respond to what children and young people are saying to us about their world — and ours?

NCEC is taking an active and developmental role in enabling

∗ the development of **thinking;**

∗ the provision of **workshops;**

∗ and the creation of multimedia **resources,** including books like this one.

Besides *Never mind the gap*, other resources already available or coming soon through *Faith in the Future* include:

∗ **Family and all that stuff** — a collection of over 20 true stories of family life and faith by well-known Christians including John Hull, Susan Staff, Anthony Reddie and Yvonne Craig. Edited by Joan King.

∗ **It's a very special day** — a book full of creative ideas, practical suggestions and thought-provoking questions to help families celebrate the Christian festivals at home.

∗ *Family Change* **series** — a series of short, accessible books addressing the unique challenges presented by family life in modern society.

∗ *Family Growth* **series** — a series of short, accessible books offering advice and resources for the parents of under-8s.

∗ *Family Options* **series** — a series of short, accessible books offering advice on the often bewildering array of choices facing the modern family.

For further information on *Faith in the Future* resources, events and workshops, or about donations and covenanting, please contact:

National Christian Education Council, 1020 Bristol Road, Selly Oak, Birmingham B29 6LB. Tel: 0121 472 4242. Fax: 0121 472 7575. E-mail: ncec@ncec.org.uk